FINAL
Arrangements 101

How and Why to Plan a Meaningful Funeral or Memorial Service, Before It's Too Late

KELLIE RICHARDSON

outskirts
press

Disclaimer

This book is intended for those with little or no experience, or knowledge in the immense value of planning for final arrangements, and other matters that must be settled when someone passes away. I am not an attorney and am not giving legal advice.

This book will by no means explain every possible scenario, nor replace the services of an attorney, estate planner, life insurance agent or funeral director. Ultimately, it is up to you to begin this process and contact the appropriate resources to ensure that all of your legal, financial and family matters are anticipated and handled appropriately.

Table of Contents

Acknowledgements

NOBODY EVER BECOMES successful on their own. As we journey through life we encounter all kinds of people, circumstances and experiences. Some things are big and obvious, and others are more subtle. Often, it's the little things along the way that we couldn't see at the time. They become big when we look back and see how the dots connected from one person, event, and situation to another.

It didn't take very long to write this book as it's been in my head for many years. I can't begin to count all of the people who, over the years, said "This is crazy! You need to write a book." If not for the hundreds of families that I served over the years, I would not have a book to write.

A big thank you to my ex-husband Ricky (mechanic extraordinaire), who put everything else on the back burner to keep my jalopy of a car running during the two years that I had a two hour commute to mortuary college. If not for you, I never would have graduated.

You know you have a great boss when he doesn't have to say or do anything in order to make you laugh. Just looking at him will do it. Thank you Dan for getting me started on the seminars that I now conduct for veterans organizations on a regular basis. The time we worked together was brief, but a huge turning point that led me to where I am now.

And last but not least, a huge thank you to Sherry and Dennis, who housed me during a six month medical ordeal, which provided me the time and space to write this book.

God leaves no stone unturned in setting up all of the events leading up to whatever it is he is using us for. I don't believe in coincidences or happenstance. It fills me with joy to know that he is in control of every detail of our lives and uses each one of us for different things. The Holy Spirit guided me through this book, and I have no doubt that it is my calling to educate and assist people with the mysterious, and often frightening process of planning for the death of our loved ones and ultimately, ourselves. I have frequently been called "the funeral lady," so I guess that's what I am.

Foreword

RECENTLY, I RECEIVED a phone call from a very angry woman who first yelled at our secretary, and then yelled at me. We were "crooks" and out to swindle people during their time of need and on and on and on. I just listened while she ranted, then began sobbing uncontrollably, and eventually hung up on me.

I have experienced this situation with dozens of other people over the years, but this was the last straw that prompted me to get busy writing this book that I had been thinking about for a long time.

We didn't do anything wrong, and the last thing we wanted to do was swindle her, or anyone else during their darkest hour. This young woman was learning the hard way what happens when someone dies without leaving any instructions, or having any of their legal affairs in order.

Her mother died unexpectedly a few days prior, at age 61. She was already taking care of her father in law who had dementia, and her husband was working sixty hour weeks, so she had no help. She was unable to access her mother's accounts and there was no will or power of attorney. They never discussed anything or made plans of any kind, and now here it was.

She didn't even have $20 to get one death certificate. When she realized she was going to have to go to court to settle her mother's estate, it was infuriating and overwhelming. We had to send her mother to another funeral home that was willing to work with her family, while they tried to come up with the funds for her cremation. It was a very sad situation that happens all too often.

It's human nature to wait until there is a crisis that directly affects us, or our family, before taking any action. We plan for a lot of things in life, but when it comes to speaking with people about death and funerals, I get a lot of "thousand yard stares" and the "deer in the headlights" looks.

Nobody wants to talk to me or others like me, until the crisis happens. I frequently receive frantic phone calls from people in situations that could have, and should have been planned for long ago.

The material in this book is too much for one, or even several conversations. It can be overwhelming and confusing. By having this book in your hands, you can read it in increments, or re-read it several times and let the information sink in before you are ready to take action. You can also read it in private. Over the years, I have spoken with many people who didn't want their family to know they were making end of life plans.

I have also met many people who were ready to make plans and a family member talked them out of it for a variety of reasons. This is a big mistake. Death is guaranteed and the sooner you deal with it, and the many issues surrounding it, the easier things will be when the time comes.

I have seen countless books about the grieving process and on death and dying. There are hundreds of books about estate planning. I have read dozens of articles about pre-planning that were written in a short, legalistic format explaining five to ten reasons to pre-plan, with one or two paragraphs explaining each reason. I have also read countless articles about the funeral home business in general. It's a unique profession.

I found very little in the way of helping people circumnavigate the industry, and get prepared so as to avoid many pitfalls and dilemmas. Over the years, I have found that the best way to help somebody understand something is to tell them relevant horror stories about other families that were in similar situations.

Instead of writing just another article about the many reasons to pre-plan, I decided to combine the concepts of pre-planning for funeral or cremation services, basic estate issues, family situations, insurance, and legal entanglements with horror stories. This subject is widely under-discussed and over-avoided.

No two people or situations are the same. Some people's to-do lists will be brief, and quick to handle. For others, it will be longer and more complicated. Hopefully, most of the concepts discussed will either not apply to you at all, or will be easy to solve. You may think your situation will be easy to handle, but then discover it's not that simple. You may learn that you have more issues than you realized. Or you may think this is going to be a big mess, but as you get each issue resolved, you find that it's not as bad as you anticipated.

Either way, it's better to get started now, than to wait until the time comes either for yourself or a loved one. Getting just some of it taken care of beforehand can make a big difference.

Introduction

IT'S A COMMON belief that you must be dead in order to go to a funeral home or cremation service. This is not the case at all. In fact, the best time to go is now, while you are still alive and able to make decisions. The younger and/or healthier you are when you begin making plans, the better off you will be over the long run. Life is good at providing us with all kinds of surprises and changes.

I strongly recommend you make your final arrangements before you die or become incapacitated. Not doing so creates its own type of grief. If you have not yet, you will eventually experience the death of someone you know, whether a family member, friend, co-worker, or business associate. Inevitably, the day will come when you yourself pass away. You can ignore it, do any number of things to postpone it, but ultimately, you can't escape it.

Views of death vary greatly from one culture, religion and person to another. This book is not about funeral rites and ceremonies from around the world, nor is it about grieving the loss of a loved one. Each person is unique and experiences a vast array of emotions and adjustments that naturally occur after a loss. The emotional grief we feel after losing a loved one is difficult enough by itself, having additional financial and legal problems makes it even worse.

There is much mystery and misconception about what happens behind the scenes in funeral homes and cemeteries. This has been capitalized on by Hollywood, often portraying funeral directors, and grave diggers as creepy and macabre. It's a common setting for many horror movies. In the media, it's big news when funeral home employees are caught doing illegal and immoral things with bodies, or skimping on services to save money. These situations are rare and happen in all industries where people are caught being unscrupulous. When these things happen, it makes the whole industry look bad.

Believe it or not, people who work at funeral homes and cemeteries are regular people. But their job is not regular. They don't just clock in, do some work and then clock out and go home. The funeral industry is a service and a ministry. They are often on call and have to sacrifice personal time because someone has died and must be tended to. The dead cannot be ignored or rescheduled.

I will share with you the many benefits of making your final arrangements as far in advance as possible. This may seem pretty straightforward but it's not. There are countless scenarios and predicaments that can arise when no plans, or inadequate plans have been made. I have experienced this many times with my own family, and with the countless number of families I have served over the years.

When a family comes to a funeral home to make arrangements, the staff immediately prepares for one of two situations: Pre-need or at-need. Pre-need is when arrangements have already been made and paid for by the decedent or their family, thus making things much faster and easier. At-need is when no prior arrangements have been made and the ensuing situation may turn out good or bad, depending on a variety of factors (mainly if the family agrees on all of the necessary decisions and has the funds to cover everything).

I want you to be a pre-need family, and save you from extra stress and expense. I will explain the many facets of this process, and help you start getting organized and prepared to complete your final arrangements. You will be able to make informed decisions, learn what you need to anticipate and plan for, avoid potential problems and feel confident when you are ready to finalize your plans at a funeral home and/or cemetery. Think of it as pre-planning to pre-plan.

I was going to include a very long chapter entitled "Horror Stories" but this could fill up a 50 part series, so I have strategically placed them throughout the book as they pertain to each subject. Also included are "happy stories" to show how certain situations can have a happy ending....provided that proper plans are made beforehand. Originally, I intended for this book to be in more of a step-by-step and checklist format, but as I began writing, I realized that the why is much more important than the how.

The how-to process is different for each person and will present itself as you begin getting your affairs in order. I am hoping you will learn from other people's mistakes in time to either fix them, or avoid them altogether. You will notice that some of the information seems redundant and I mention certain things in more than one chapter. This means that it's very important, and that certain concepts can have more than one outcome depending on the circumstances. What turns out horrible in one situation, turns out great in another.

You are probably wondering what my credentials are that qualify me to discuss this subject. In a nutshell, I have an A.A.S in Mortuary Science and have worked on and off since 1998, at eight funeral homes and one transportation service. I have done everything from embalming, cremating, cleaning up after autopsies, 2 am pick-ups, meeting with families and planning services, administration, selling pre-need arrangements and transporting the deceased to other towns, cemeteries and airports. But rest assured these are not my claims to fame as my passion runs much deeper than a list of tasks and credentials, otherwise I would not be writing this book.

During the periods that I wasn't working at a funeral home, I was not off the hook. I dealt with the terminal illnesses and deaths of several family members, in addition to the deaths of several childhood and military friends. I received a steady stream of calls from friends and relatives dealing with a death in their family. I accompanied several people to funeral homes because they wanted to pre-plan but did not want to go alone, or get duped into overspending.

My personal experience started when I was very young. My

family was very adept at visiting funeral homes. We had one to three funerals a year, about every year for over thirty years....it all started when my great-grandmother died on my twelfth birthday. I probably would have lost count years ago but I have all the service folders in a shoe box.

The older relatives died naturally and we celebrated the long, full life that they lived but we have also experienced numerous un-natural, unexpected, young deaths in our family. Our motto became "We don't die, we get killed." When I was twenty six, we had a typical year for our family, two deaths in two months. We already used the same funeral home several other times so we knew what to do. They didn't have to explain anything to us. My mom joked that we should just buy the place since we were the family keeping it in business.

After I flew back to the Midwest, I could not stop thinking about it. Who in their right mind would work at a funeral home? The peo-ple I met there seemed "normal," but are they? On a whim, I began researching how someone goes about working at a funeral home. I learned that the nearest mortuary school was just two hours away. I called for information, and was delighted to learn that the program qualified for veteran education benefits. Several months later, there I was. I fit right in with the others, made the honor roll and knew that I was in the right place.

The next two years were a huge investment. I got up at four am to make the two hour drive to be in school for six hours a day, three days a week. During the other two days and weekends, I had about eight hours of studying to do in addition to volunteering part time at two funeral homes. My life completely changed for the better. No more going out or social engagements, and even no more yard work. I turned off the TV, changed into a new business ward robe, and gained a new purpose in life.

There were about a hundred people in the program and I was one of the younger ones at twenty seven. Most of the other students were middle aged and already had other degrees, mainly business and biology. There were many veterans and people who had already retired from their first career, and were now working in the funeral industry as a second career, or side job.

Subjects covered included anatomy and physiology, organic chemistry, micro-biology, pathology and embalming. In addition, we learned about the grieving process, funeral rites and customs from around the world, business management, business writing, mortuary law, and the history of modern funeral directing. Simultaneously, we had to complete a two-semester practicum at a local funeral home. Most of us worked without pay, and it was basically a pre-internship. You had to be an intern before you could be an intern.

We attended special seminars with guest speakers, went on field trips to the medical examiner's office, vault and headstone companies, and a casket manufacturing facility. We shared and discussed our work experiences, and continuously learned about health laws and legal issues that are specific to the funeral home industry.

Upon graduation, we then had to pass a comprehensive exam. It lasted several hours and not everyone passed. Before being approved to work as an apprentice, each person had to pass a background check, get fingerprinted and register with the state. This is kind of like having a learners permit to drive. You can perform various duties as an embalmer and funeral director, as long as you are supervised by someone who is already licensed.

Each quarter, every apprentice had to fill out a report showing how many people they have embalmed, how many families they have met with and various other duties. After one year, if the state decided that you fulfilled all requirements, then you could take another comprehensive test to obtain your real license(s). Many people had to travel to other cities to complete these tests, as they are not offered in all areas.

There is only a few dozen mortuary schools in the entire country. For most people, it's not a popular line of work to pursue. A handful of people stay in the business long term, and everyone else comes and goes. It's a huge responsibility and commitment that is not easy or comfortable.

Looking back almost twenty years later, I can honestly say that this was one of the biggest and most difficult challenges I ever endured.

I tried to permanently quit a few times but no matter how hard I tried to stay away from it, or what other vocation I tried to take up, I always somehow ended up back in it. I didn't have to go after it. Most of the jobs found me through a strange series of events. I finally took the hint, and know this is my calling.

So remember when you go to any funeral home, that the people working there did not just get hired off the street. It takes a special type of person to even want to work at a funeral home. School is just the beginning, the continuing education and licensing requirements never end.

The funeral home industry is regulated at the national and state level, and by OSHA (Occupational Safety and Health Administration), and carries additional liabilities and ethical issues that most other businesses do not.

As with anything else, people who work at funeral homes have their strengths and weaknesses, some are really adept at embalming but don't like making arrangements with families, and vice versa. At some funeral homes, each person is capable of, and often required, to do anything and everything as needed. At others they work in teams on separate aspects of the process.

Larger funeral homes will often have a removal team or contract with a service that goes out and picks up the deceased, another team that embalms and prepares them, another team that meets with the families and arranges the services, and another team that operates the crematory. And of course administration, even death will not save you from paperwork. I will elaborate more on the intricate workings of funeral homes throughout the book.

My strengths and joys were working with the families before and after the services. I loved talking to people about the various things they needed to decide on and plan for. Some had prior experience with family members, though most did not and were shocked at how many options were available. Many were even more shocked to learn about all of the other issues that needed to be considered.

I enjoyed visiting with families after all of the services were over, usually while delivering death certificates. After the family and friends were gone, many people would open up and vent. I just listened. I didn't really enjoy embalming or being on call. It never failed, as long as I just sat around, nothing would happen. As soon as I was about to fall asleep, or start doing laundry, a call would come in. It was all a very worthwhile experience and I do not regret any of it, but I just was a lot more comfortable during the before and after stages.

In my most recent stint, my boss and I conducted many funeral planning seminars for local veteran organizations, and I spoke on several radio programs targeted to veterans. I was frequently contacted by frantic family members whose loved one had, or was about to pass away and they didn't know what to do.

I was able to incorporate the funeral home job into the many veteran events and groups that I have been a part of for many years. I attended a lot of trade shows and resource fairs. Pretty soon, almost all of my clients were veterans and their families. Since leaving my job in pre-need sales, these calls and seminar requests have increased so this is my new direction.

This book applies to everyone, but one chapter is for veterans and anyone who will be making plans for one. There are unique issues and options that don't apply to the general population. It's important to learn this information before you begin making plans, as it will most likely alter whatever you have in mind.

There is a wealth of information online, though nothing can replace good old fashioned face to face meetings. I will not be using technical information, statistics, or industry jargon, etc. This book is not intended for industry insiders. They already know all of this and can easily elaborate. Above all, this is not a research project. All of the information and stories are from my own experience serving countless families, including my own family and friends.

As you read this book, keep these three things in mind.....

1. *In most circumstances, it's not what you do or don't HAVE, but WHO is handling it and HOW it's handled, that determines the outcome of any given situation.*
2. *I am not telling you what kind of service to plan, I am telling you to plan some kind of service.*
3. *I am not telling you what to do, I am telling you to do something.*

CHAPTER **1**

Myths and Misconceptions

OF ALL OF the industries people work in, none is more misunderstood, and falsely portrayed as the funeral home industry is. This chapter could become a book all on its own. I have heard it all, and seen all the movies and TV shows. Some of the scenarios depicted have some truth to them, but by and large, they are not accurate portrayals of what goes on in the funeral home industry.

I have spoken with people who truly believe that funeral home employees mutilate bodies, steal their jewelry and dental gold, mix up their ashes or bury them in the wrong grave and an endless array of other unpleasant things.

My advice to these people is to stop watching TV and stop reading tabloids. I have seen some horrible, yet hilarious stories in a few certain "news" papers depicting funeral home and cemetery employees as greedy, sinister crooks. I will clarify and explain a few of the common misconceptions.

I have also seen the real news documentaries involving funeral home and cemetery staff that were caught in scandals of various types, such as operating without proper licenses, burying someone in the wrong grave, pretending to cremate people while actually dumping them in the woods, and the one funeral home that buried their trash in people's caskets to save on the garbage bill.

As I mentioned in the introduction, these things have happened in the past and they become big news. These incidents are very rare. Please do not accept these stories as normal or common. Every industry has its bad apples that make the whole industry look bad.

Recently, I watched a crime documentary about a young man who murdered his neighbor. He had previously worked at a funeral home, and it was made to sound as though that somehow contributed to his state of mind and behavior leading up to the murder. He had worked there very briefly and did not work with the families or on any of the bodies. He assisted with janitorial and grounds keeping duties.

I have seen many similar situations get portrayed in a similar manner. It's very misleading.

Most funeral homes and cremation services are upstanding, legitimate businesses that go to great lengths to care for the dead, and serve their families with respect and dignity. Though I have worked with some people who weren't very pleasant to be around, none of them ever did anything illegal or immoral, nor blatantly disrespected a family.

Dead Bodies Do Not Sit Up

The biggest myth pertains to dead bodies sitting up. This is completely false. Sitting up requires movement; movement requires energy. Dead people no longer have any energy and that's why they're dead. It's physiologically impossible. I have heard all kinds of things from people about how their friends' brother's girlfriend's grandmother sat up during her funeral....No, she did not.

When someone dies in a hospital or other facility, the staff has to do the usual paperwork and reports. Often, the family stays in the room with their loved one for a time while this is happening. By the time the funeral home is called, they have been dead at least two to three hours.

For those sent to the medical examiner's office, it can be several days before they are released to a funeral home. Sometimes when a body arrives at a funeral home quickly, say within two hours, there may still be some muscle twitching here and there because the entire body does not die all at once. But the body itself is not moving.

Most of the stories you hear about dead people sitting up are witnessed by first responders. When someone has just had a fatal event, often during CPR, the person may make a final "jolt" or gasp for air just before they die. If you want to hear more about this, ask a paramedic or other medical personnel.

Dental Gold

The second common myth involves dental gold. Modern dental gold is pretty much worthless outside its intended purpose. It is not pure and has no dollar value. If it did, everyone would have it removed, including me. Several dozen people have asked me about this over the years.

Even if someone did want it removed from a loved one's mouth after they died, it would cost a lot more than the funeral. They would have to hire a forensic dentist, who would then have to go the funeral home to perform the procedure. I have never seen, or heard of this happening. In addition, I have never seen any dental gold survive the cremation process.

One family I assisted tried for years to convince their mother to make pre-arrangements. She would not do it because she had so much "money in her mouth" and they could just have it removed and melted down for payment. They believed her. When we sat down with them, they were quite dismayed to learn that this was not going to happen. They ended up putting her services on several credit cards.

Theft

In some incidents, a funeral home employee has stolen jewelry and other items from a body. But the truth is, more often than not, these items are stolen by family members. During viewings, it's easy to slip a ring off, or remove a necklace from the decedent when nobody is looking.

To avoid false allegations and legal problems, many funeral homes have hidden cameras placed above the casket during viewings. This way there is no argument over who stole Aunt Edna's diamonds. I have never seen anyone I worked with steal anything.

Great measures are taken to ensure that all personal items are either returned to the family, or placed on, or with the decedent.

Most funeral homes have plastic bags, like the ones you get at the hospital. A list is made of all personal items, which items stay on the body and which ones get returned to the family.

If there is any chance of a problem or doubt, many funeral homes take pictures of certain items such as jewelry, wallets, cash, etc.

One funeral home I worked at would make copies of any cash that was used for payment or for memorial donations. If someone donated $50, was it one bill or two twenty's and a ten? This way, there were no mistakes and the funeral home stayed above reproach.

I once embalmed a man that had over seven hundred dollars in his pocket. I immediately informed the funeral director that was to meet with his family. We made copies of each bill and recorded them onto a list of items to be returned to his family. It was then placed in a labeled bag, and locked in a safe until the family signed for it.

Mutilations

While working in this industry, I have never known anyone who acted in a way that would cause harm to a body. From the people who pick up and transport the body, to the embalmers, the funeral director and other staff assisting with the service, great care is taken to protect the body from anything that would cause injury or loss.

Additionally, funeral homes do not sell body parts on the black market. By the time they receive a body, it's too late to recover any usable organs. Most organ donation procedures take place at the hospital or the medical examiner's office.

The only exception I saw was cornea donations, that were removed by an embalmer with special certification to do so, and a retired coroner who removed the brains of people with Alzheimer's, and took them to a medical school for research. Both procedures are completely legitimate and authorized.

It's completely different from other organ removals that will be used for live transplant, such as hearts and livers.

The most ridiculous thing I have ever heard, by not one, but several people, is the belief that funeral home staff straps bodies to tables, tilts them up, and then pokes holes in the bottom of their feet to let the blood drain out. I must have missed that horror movie. Not even close.

Misidentification

Most funeral homes, especially larger, busier ones have a very strict chain of custody. It starts with an identification bracelet being placed on the decedent's ankle, similar to the kind you get at the hospital. Every person who moves or handles the body must fill out a form with exact details.

From the initial pick up, placement in the refrigeration unit at the funeral home, the embalmer, then the funeral director in charge of their service, and the driver who transports them to another location such as a cemetery, church, another town or the airport, all must take great care to ensure that nobody is misidentified. The decedents paperwork stays with them at all times.

In addition, nobody is ever just "dropped off" at a cemetery or church. The casket is attended to at all times. I have spent countless hours at cemeteries, guarding a casket until the family arrives and staying until the casket was lowered. Sometimes it was lowered with the family present, other times they preferred to leave beforehand.

Either way I had to stay until the casket was completely lowered into the ground. Not half way, not when the grounds crew said "we got it." I have stood outside in the rain and snow, in very hot and freezing temperatures to make sure that nothing happened while waiting for the family to arrive, or leave, and then for the grounds crew to arrive.

The situation was similar at churches. I spent many hours sitting with caskets that were taken to a church several hours before the service. Even though the church staff was present, we could not leave and assume that everything would be okay. There is no room for error in risking any possibility of anything happening to the casket or the person inside.

Cremation

Many people have shared their fears with me about what happens during cremation. It's illegal to use a crematory for anything other than a human. They do not burn garbage or cremate pets and there is room for one person only. Nobody is stacked or doubled up in any way. There are many pet cemeteries and cremation services around the nation that cremate pets in a crematory similar to a regular one. But they are for pets only.

It is also unlawful to burn out-of-commission or retired flags in a crematory. Since flags should never be just thrown away, or burned in a regular fire without a ceremony, some people assume that they must be burned in more dignified way, such as at a crematory. Check with your local veterans or government organizations to find out where, and how, flags are to be properly disposed of in your area.

At the crematory, more measures are taken to ensure the correct identity. A review is made of their full legal name to ensure that it matches the name on the bracelet. Some funeral homes take pictures, and others have ID viewings where a family or friend confirms, in person, that it is indeed the right person. The paperwork is attached outside the metal door. A metal disc with an identification number is placed inside with the body. Afterwards, the disc is attached to, or placed inside the plastic bag containing the ashes.

In recent years, it has become popular to fill a cardboard or cloth pod with human ashes and plant a tree in it. It's implied that the ashes will make the tree grow. What a wonderful way to memorialize some-one, except that it doesn't work. Once you are cremated, there are no longer any nutrients left in your bones or ashes.

The tree is going to grow because of the soil, water and sunlight, just like all the other plants on earth. Not because your ashes are feeding it. It's still a nice thing to plant a tree in someone's memory, so don't feel too deflated if this is your wish. Just know that it's not you or your loved one making it grow.

Price Fixing

Prior to 1984, most funeral homes were independent, private or family owned, therefore were pretty much free to operate as they pleased. Since then, many new laws have been created to regulate the industry. (If you want the details, look up Federal Trade Commission, Funeral Rule). There were many issues covered, but one important one involved prices.

Prior to this, a funeral home could make up things as they went, meaning that they could charge one family a certain price for a casket and then charge another family more or less for the same casket.

This was great if you were family or friends with the funeral home owner, but not so great if he didn't know you or was in a bad mood that day. This practice is now illegal.

In addition, funeral homes no longer keep funds used for pre-arranged services in their facility. The money is kept in either a trust, or handled by the insurance company that provides the coverage. This way, if a funeral home shuts down for any reason, the money is untouched and safe. In the past, there were some incidents where a funeral home owner collected payments for many years, from many people and then shut down the funeral home and fled. There was no way for anyone to recover their money.

It's All a Racket!

I have heard no end of complaints from people about how the funeral home industry is a big rip off and they are out to swindle people who are grieving. Maybe some are, and I have known a handful of funeral home employees who have not provided very good customer service to the families they served. I am going to explain pre-planning from several angles in this book but for now consider this: Did you marry your spouse the same day that you met them? Would you buy a car without looking under the hood or test driving it? Would you buy a house without first having it inspected?

Chances are you date first, test drive, inspect and research whatever it is that you are considering either buying or getting involved with. Doing so won't guarantee that every detail will turn out exactly as you expect, but for the most part, you feel pretty prepared and confident that you are making the right choice.

The same principles apply to pre-planning for your final expenses and other legal matters. Dying is the equal but opposite event to being born. For most people, welcoming a baby is a joyous event. The expenses and pains are soon outweighed by the cuteness and fresh hope of a new life. But mention death and funerals and people run away as quickly as possible. It's expensive to be born and it's expensive to die.

How can you expect the staff at a funeral home to magically know everything about your recently deceased loved one when you have not prepared anything? They can't help write an obituary or prepare a death certificate by guessing or assuming.

They can't put together a nice service if they don't have the necessary information and cooperation from the survivors. They cannot prevent family fights. It's not their fault that a family doesn't have the funds set aside for this reason. It's not their fault that the county charges so much for each certified copy of a death certificate.

The real "racket" is that too many people remain uninformed, unprepared and fearful of the unknown. Many people don't even think about, let alone plan for the inevitable. When the time comes, there is all kinds of emotional reactions, turmoil, trauma and drama. The bulk of which can be anticipated and prevented, with proper planning. Funeral Directors are often on the receiving end of emotional outbursts, and all kinds of accusations that are simply the result of people not having made prior plans. Ultimately, it is your responsibility to take the appropriate actions necessary to complete this process.

In Summary

By becoming informed and taking the time to anticipate, investigate, and process the information, you will be better able to take appropriate action to avoid problems for both yourself and the survivors that you will leave behind.

There is an array of other fears, stereotypes, and misconceptions about funeral homes and crematories. As you read this book, please clear your mind of these or from whatever horror movie you just watched. It doesn't work that way, and when you go to make arrangements for yourself or for someone else, you will find that there is nothing creepy or sinister going on.

Funeral homes and cremation services are licensed, insured, regulated, inspected, audited and investigated just like all other businesses.

CHAPTER 2

What Is Pre-Planning and Why Should I Do It?

WHEN SOMEONE DIES, whether expected or not, it's a very stressful time and many people aren't able to think clearly. Many decisions have to be made. These decisions can be even more difficult when a family is grieving and unprepared. I would like to share a few vivid memories that are permanently embedded into my mind.

Horror Story

A man died without making any arrangements or leaving instructions. He left behind seven adult children from two marriages. His wife was in a nursing home, unaware of his passing. When the family arrived, we could tell they had already been arguing. You could cut the tension with a knife.

The kids from the first marriage wanted him buried in a blue metal casket, wearing his church suit. They were thinking of a traditional service, just like the one their mom had when they were young. The kids and step-kids from the second marriage wanted him in a wood casket wearing his fishing vest. They wanted the service to be more upbeat and personalized, displaying their fathers fishing gear and other mementos that reflected the life he lived.

A few verbal jabs escalated into a full on war. One of the biological sons reminded the step son that he and his sisters "didn't count" and the fight was on.....literally. The arrangement office turned into a boxing ring. They were punching, head slamming, and kicking each other around the room. The funeral director and another son pulled them apart and dragged them down the hall and out the door, both of them still yelling and threatening each other. The fight resumed in the parking lot.

Meanwhile, two of the sisters were yelling at each other over who had spent more time with, and taken care of him. Another staff member came out and announced that the police were on their way, only then did they calm down enough to get in their cars and leave. With the chaos gone, the funeral director returned to the arrangement room.

Only one daughter and step daughter had remained quiet and calm through all of this. Since they were the only ones with the funds to pay for his service anyway, they made arrangements without the others present. Their dad got his fishing themed funeral and the two sons that started the fight ended up not even coming. Though most families do not get into physical altercations, the strife is common. All of this could have been avoided if their father had made plans, and informed his family of those plans.

Happy Story

A middle aged couple asked us for some information because they were planning to get all of their financial and legal matters in order before they retired. We gave them some brochures and a planning guide. A few days later, they came back.

They spoke with her parents, who had made their arrangements with us a few years prior and still had about two years of payments due. Money was getting tight and they were struggling.

They decided that they would take over her parent's payments in addition to making their own arrangements. She then called her father in law, who had purchased a plot several years ago when his wife died, but did not yet have any funeral plans and no way to pay for it at the time. After a family meeting, they decided it would be best to just take care of everyone at once. The collective bill for all five people including cemetery costs was close to $30k.

This couple stayed at their jobs for another year to pay for this. What a huge relief. They retired with peace of mind and a huge expense off their plate. Four months after making the last payment, her father died and a year later her husband's father died. In a perfect world, every family would plan like this.

Pre-planning is just that. You anticipate, decide, and record your wishes and instructions, so your survivors will know what to do after you die. When I say pre-plan, I am not just referring to the actual signing of a contract at a funeral home or cemetery. For some people, it could simply mean writing their wishes in a notebook.

For others, it could mean talking to their family, though I strongly recommend that everyone records them in some way. Each one of us has a different family and financial situation. *The way you have your estate and final arrangements planned and recorded will have a huge impact on your survivors, either good or bad.*

Some families have the same type of service for all their members and never deviate from them, so there is no need to leave special instructions. Some people have ample funds to cover whatever may come and do not desire or feel the need to make prior arrangements. If you fall into one of these categories, you are rare. Regardless, make sure your family knows what to do after your passing.

I remember one very large family I worked with. The matriarch died at age 98. Her friends and relatives came together to celebrate her life. They picked out a beautiful pink casket, a matching vault, lots of flowers, and had a full traditional service complete with an open casket viewing. Everyone pitched in to cover all the costs. It was a festive event that doubled as a reunion, as is so common nowadays. After the service, the procession headed out to the cemetery where she would be buried next to her parents, and then back to the church for a large reception.

A few months later, while cleaning out her home, a grandson found the notebook. It was at the bottom of a drawer in the dining room covered with cloth napkins. Their grandmother had written down everything she did and did not want after her passing.

She wanted a white casket, and to be buried next to her cousin that she was very close to all her life. She had already purchased the plot many years before.

There were several other things that she had wanted that were different than what actually happened. She never told anyone about her plans or where the notebook was. Judging from the other entries, they guessed it to be about twenty years old. Though it was too late, she still had a wonderful service. This situation influenced her children to start thinking about their own plans. Many families do not fare so well.

I met with a woman in her early 70's that was sitting in our lobby. She accompanied a friend to help with arrangements after his father died. She was on a mission to get everyone she knew to get all of their arrangements made as far in advance as possible. She told me the story of her parents. One Saturday afternoon, without warning, her father died. Everyone was in shock and didn't know what to do.

He never discussed his wishes with anyone, including his wife. It just never came up. When the rest of her siblings arrived, it was agreed that he would be buried and they would contribute to the costs later that month. She and her husband put $8k on several credit cards. They were banking on getting money from the other siblings.

Meanwhile, she tried to convince her mother to make her arrangements, and get all of her other legal matters in order so they would not have this kind of stress again. Her mother assured her that they had taken care of their legal affairs years ago. Several months later, she too died unexpectedly.

The family assembled again and it was decided that their mom was to have the same service their father had. The siblings promised they were working on getting the funds, which they still owed from the first funeral. Again, this couple took out a loan to cover the expenses.

They now had funeral debt of almost $16k. To make matters worse, it was discovered that her parent's finances were in shambles.

They had very little money and their life insurance policies had lapsed years earlier. Their will looked to be several decades old and had not been signed or notarized.

Long story short, this couple had to cancel their anniversary vacation, sell the motor home and re-finance the house. Then they almost got divorced, her husband was ready to retire and hit the road and it was all cancelled because of her family. Her siblings never paid her. Her parent's estate went into probate, and it took almost a year to get the house sold and everything settled. They barely broke even.

Now this woman wanted to share her bad experience with everyone she knew, and encourage them to not be like her family. She would have been a great marketing agent.

Funeral homes get a lot of their business from situations like this. Many people experience firsthand how exhausting and complicated it can be to make someone else's arrangements, and then have to settle their estate afterwards. It's common for family members to return some time later to make their own arrangements, so their kids don't have to endure what they did with their own parents. Some people make their arrangements and then talk their other family members into it during the next family gathering. Many people will step up if someone else close to them has already done so.

Peace of Mind

It's comforting for everyone involved to know that these matters have already been settled. If you have made them for yourself, you can relax knowing that when you die, most everything is already decided and your children will not have to make major decisions. It also negates family feuds over what type of disposition and service to plan. It's a huge burden lifted for everyone.

Aside from the fact that you could die tomorrow, you could also become incapacitated and not be able to make decisions. You could have a stroke, develop dementia, become brain damaged, or need to be on life support. These situations can cause similar legal problems and it's imperative that you also have your last will and testament, power of attorney and advance directives in place. I will discuss this further in a later chapter.

I personally benefitted from this when my mother passed away. She was a very meticulous person who was always planning and making lists, she saved every receipt and document from everything that could possibly be an issue at some point. Several years prior, she made all of her final arrangements which consisted of a direct cremation and then placement in a family plot.

She paid for everything, down to the smallest detail. In fact, she over planned. The cemetery package included an urn so she picked out a pink one, which we used. The funeral home package also included an urn, since it was paid for, the funeral director let me pick one right off the display wall. I chose a patriotic themed urn and donated it to a local veteran's group.

She also updated all of her legal and financial affairs. When she knew that she had only a few months left, she met with her stockbroker and insurance agent to make sure that everything was current and accurate. She signed her car title over to me and then called the firm that handled her retirement funds. Once all of this was taken care of, she was able to relax and spend her last two months visiting with family and friends.

When she passed away, her estate was completely settled in less than one month with no attorneys, court proceedings, or any other red tape. She didn't just get up one day and decide that doing all of this would be a good idea. It was the result of several previous deaths in our family that were not planned beforehand.

Family Matters

If you will be making plans for someone else, namely a parent, don't wait until their death is imminent or has already occurred. Unfortunately, this is when most people learn the hard way that there is so much that needs to be done, and things are not always as simple as they seem. Talk to them now and find out if all of their affairs are in order. It's common for older people to forget about things, such as insurance policies, or how many years have passed since they wrote their will, and who they appointed as power of attorney.

If it's been "a while," it's time to find it all and update it. This may be easier said than done, I have talked with many people who were trying to do this but their parents would not cooperate, or were positive that it had been handled long ago. This is why I implore you to start getting organized now. It may take a while to figure out everything that needs to be updated and taken care of. This is when a lot of family fights start over who will be in charge, and who is entitled to this and that.

Horror Story

I remember one family that didn't make any arrangements or check on anything because their mother had promised them that she took care of everything many years ago, after her husband died. They believed her. When she passed away, they came in to finalize her plans that she had already paid for. It was then discovered that she had indeed made her funeral plans and made several payments, but only for about six months.

Her policy lapsed and she had only a few hundred dollars in her account. Her three children had to pare down her service quite a bit and put over $4k on several credit cards, just a few weeks before Christmas. They also discovered that her life insurance policy had lapsed years earlier.

If their mother had kept up on the payments, she would have had a full service for about $1200. Now it was almost four times that amount for just a basic service.

When the oldest daughter came in several days later to pick up the death certificates, she told us that her will was not valid. She also owed property taxes and several other bills that they did not know about. They were not happy.

Another Horror Story

Another family ended up in probate court because their mother put her middle son in charge of everything. He was the power of attorney and the executor of her estate. He had lived nearby, been an accountant for years and knew how to handle these things. There was just one problem.....he died in a car accident five years prior. She never updated anything after his death. Her car title was still in her husband's name and she had not renewed the tabs in three years. They also thought she had a life insurance policy but it turned out to be a small policy on their father that lapsed many years ago.

Our parents and grand-parents lived in a time when life was much simpler than it is now. Things did not change as often, or as drastic as they do now. Many older people who took care of something, or think they did many years ago may not realize that it is no longer valid. Handwritten wills and instructions for a variety of things are no longer accepted in most cases.

In addition, people often behave themselves in front of certain family members, namely parents and grandparents. When they die, the manure hits the fan. The truth comes out and all kinds of problems and battles occur. Men fight over dad's tools, guns and vehicles. Women fight over mom's jewelry, wedding china, and silver tea sets. I don't need to even mention money.

People that are usually reasonable and stable can become the complete opposite after a death, or even before. Many elderly people don't want to believe that their family will fight over their things and money. *I will mention more than once that family is the main source of conflict, estate fraud and theft.*

If you would like to hear more about this, just ask any attorney who specializes in elder law, anyone who works at a nursing home, assisted living facility or for your local Adult Protective Services agency.

Don't Pass the Burden

Another common reason is that people don't want to pass the burden down to their children or other family members. When you die, someone has to pay for it and most of the time that somebody is your children. I have heard this from the vast majority of people who I assisted with pre-arrangements.

They feel responsible to take care of this now, not only to save their family the expenses but also to avoid having to make major decisions. Doing so avoids a lot of strife. It may not seem like a great gift idea but believe me it is. If there is ANY chance that your family will not be able to afford, or to cooperatively decide on your final arrangements, then it's the best gift you can give them.

A Very Happy Story

I recently worked with an elderly man, ninety seven years old and sharp as a tack. He had an unusual situation and knew that he better get it together. He had a large family, some in our town, and more in his hometown, seven hours away. He planned for two funerals. The first one would be in our town. This included a full traditional service with an open casket viewing.

He picked out his casket, folders, flowers, music and every other detail. After his service, he would be flown back to his hometown where the other side of his family would have a graveside service. He already paid for the plots years earlier when his wife died. Additionally, he also set money aside to pay for the flight, his obituaries in two newspapers and his death certificates, and any other incidental that may occur.

The reason he did all of this is because he is very wealthy and the family fights started long ago. He knew it would be family Armageddon if he didn't, so he had every detail of his estate covered in an iron-clad will.

He appointed one grand-daughter as his power of attorney and executrix of his estate. He didn't trust anyone else and went to great lengths to protect her, and his wishes.

He brought her to the funeral home so I could walk her through everything she needed to know. I gave her additional materials that we normally didn't give to families until after the services were over. When the time came, she would save a lot of time and trouble by already knowing where to go and what to do. She was very relieved to learn all of this information. This is a rare situation but a great example of someone doing the right thing. If only everyone had this sense of urgency and was honest with themselves about their family situation.

Pay for It Now

Another common financial scenario I have seen many times is that people want to pay for it while they have the money. Many people, after settling their loved ones estate, receive an inheritance from them. They use this money to make their own arrangements because they don't know what the future will bring. They cannot afford it with their regular income so some kind of inheritance or other windfall allows them to do so.

I have one close friend that did this after losing both of his parents in a house fire. Needless to say, he was overwhelmed and unable to think clearly. When he finally got their estate settled, he made his own arrangements and updated all of his other legal issues as well. He is now the legal guardian of his adult sister with special needs. She always lived with their parents, but thankfully, was not at home that night. Instead of having fun with his parent's money, he used it to make sure that all of her needs would be met in the event of his passing, or any other situation that would render him unable to care for her.

I have met with many other people who felt the need to take care of this before it was either too late, or made difficult.

One couple knew that their income would shrink after they retired so they made plans to have it all paid off before then. Another couple sold their boat that they used about once a year, so they could pay for their plots. Another couple made some adjustments to their life style so they could get their house paid off early, and then use that money to get their final expenses paid off too.

Make YOUR Wishes Known

Another major reason is simply that you want your services to reflect you, and how you want to be remembered. If you do not make

19

your wishes known, your family will just do "whatever" and it may not be anything close to what you've envisioned.

I have spoken with many people over the years that really didn't care what their family will do with them because they will be dead and gone.

For others, it does matter. As I mentioned earlier, a major source of strife amongst survivors is whether to bury or cremate. If you absolutely do not want to be viewed or embalmed, you need to make it known. If you absolutely want to be cremated and then scattered in a particular place, then you need to make it known. Don't assume that your family will automatically know what to do, or remember something you mentioned several years ago. Even worse, your family may do something "cheaper," or nothing at all, instead of honoring your wishes.

I recently spoke with a young man in his mid-twenties who is an avid backpacker. He wants to be cremated and at least half of his ashes scattered in a particular lake. There is no way anyone in his family will be physically able to get up to the remote area, so I convinced him that he needs to write all of his wishes down and talk to his family about them.

They will most likely have a regular memorial service for him in town, and then arrangements will have to be made for someone fit enough to carry and scatter his ashes in the lake. His family would otherwise have no idea what he wanted, or have any way to make it happen according to his wishes.

Happy Story

One woman I assisted had been a school teacher for many years, she enjoyed it but it was not her true passion. Her real passion was quilting. Over the years, she made thousands of them. She donated them to people in nursing homes, hospitals, and crisis nurseries. She was involved in many community service projects, taught quilting and sewing classes, and received many awards for her community involvement and charity work.

Much of this work was done quietly. She knew that when she

passed away, most people would remember her from school. She wanted to make sure that the rest of the story was told so she planned out her funeral in detail. She wrote most of her obituary and eulogy, and assembled a pile of photograph's to be made into a slideshow. She was afraid that her family would not take the time to "cover everything" and that her service would be bland.

Unforeseen Circumstances

The entire process is made easier for the survivors of those who plan ahead. For some people, there is no consolation whether plans were made or not. It may feel safe to assume that you will live into your later years. If you don't live to be one hundred, you will probably at least make it to retirement. It's presumably expected to die from natural causes as you get older. You may envision living to be a ripe old age and dying peacefully, in your sleep or surrounded by loved ones. I hope this is how it happens for you.

Until there is an unexpected or tragic death in the family, it's not something most people think about it. Most people don't want to. They are young, healthy and bullet proof, until it happens. I have seen death occur at all ages from many causes such as car wrecks, suicides, homicides, household accidents, cleaning guns, slipping on ice, electrocutions, drowning's and of course the usual culprits of cancer, stroke and heart attack. Aside from suicides or imminently expected deaths, nobody plans to die on any given day.

Nobody plans for a post-surgical wound to get infected. Nobody plans for their dad to fall off the roof while putting up the Christmas lights. Nobody plans to have their car slide into a river. Nobody plans to have a heart attack while doing 65 on the freeway. Nobody plans to get crushed under a beam at work. Nobody ever plans to be in the wrong place at the wrong time.

The Worst Horror Story

The worst cause of death is of course, homicide. The saddest situation I ever encountered was that of a woman who was a victim of mistaken identity. One weekend, she traveled to another town to do some Christmas shopping with an old friend. On the way back from the mall, they stopped by the house of her friend's sister.

A huge, rowdy party was underway. She just finished eating and was taking her plate to the garbage. Suddenly, another woman walked up and shot her several times. The shooter had just found out that her boyfriend was dating another woman and planned to leave her. Another friend told her what the other woman looked like. Without asking or confirming, she just walked up to the first woman who fit the description and killed her.

This young woman died on the kitchen floor at a stranger's house, while outside, her car was full of Christmas presents for her four year old daughter, and two young nephews. She was just thirty three, and recently diagnosed with MS. I did not usually get emotionally involved in the many families I served, but this one deeply affected me. She was short, chunky, and kept her long brown hair pulled back in a ponytail, just like me.

It took everything out of me to get through the arrangement meeting with her family. She was well loved by her family, friends and co-workers, and was a wonderful mother. During the previous two months, she worked overtime so she could provide her daughter and nephew's with a nice Christmas.

Unfortunately, she ended up in the wrong place at the wrong time.....if only they hadn't stopped at the party. I followed the story over the next year. The shooter went to prison and the boyfriend married the other woman who was the intended target. To add more salt to the wound, the shooter was also seeing other partners but it wasn't okay that her boyfriend was. This young woman had never even met this couple. How can you possibly plan for something like this?

In Summary

Regardless of your family or financial situation, getting your final arrangements and other legal matters in order will reduce or eliminate many additional problems. After you pass away, many things happen and decisions need to be made.

This is a very difficult process on its own, and will be a lot worse when your survivors don't know what you wanted and/or are unable to pay for it. If you think that you can't afford it then you can't afford to ignore it.

Your family will not be able to ignore it when the time comes.

CHAPTER 3

Veterans

JUST ABOUT EVERYONE knows at least one person that is a veteran. I can think of only two people that I have ever met who had no veteran connections at all. No family, friends, co-workers etc. Whether you are a veteran or a family member, or someone who will be making plans for one, the information in this chapter is very important and will probably change the plans you have, or think you have…or more accurately that you don't have because of the common misconception that the government pays for final arrangements.

I will elaborate later in this chapter, which is a brief overview of some issues that pertain to veterans. You will undoubtedly have more questions and concerns, most of which will be covered in subsequent chapters, as the rest of this book also applies to veterans.

Active Duty vs. Veteran Death

In regards to burial benefits, there is a big difference between the death of a service man or woman, still on active duty, and that of a person who has previously served and now has veteran status. When someone dies while serving, be it from combat, accidents, natural causes or from suicide, the government usually provides for most, or all of the final arrangements for this person. They are still on Uncle Sam's clock. Once discharged, this all goes away. The government provides only very limited benefits for veterans who meet certain criteria.

Overview of Eligibility and Criteria

The only part of your final arrangements that's free is burial or inurnment in a national or state veterans cemetery, a flag, a marker or headstone, and certain transportation expenses. (Flags and markers are provided to those using private cemeteries as well).

By using a veteran cemetery, you can save thousands of dollars, especially if your spouse will be buried with you.

Whichever cemetery you plan to use, contact them now for information regarding eligibility requirements, and the application process. Most honorably discharged veterans and their spouses qualify. However, there are some exceptions, such as having a criminal record. Even if you served honorably, if you later commit certain serious offenses, you lose the right to be buried in a veteran cemetery. This applies to only a handful of people, but there are other situations and categories of veterans who may not qualify.

Some National Guard and Reservists qualify, if they were ever called to active or federal service. State service by itself does not qualify. In addition, anyone who receives a dishonorable discharge does not qualify. If the veteran received an "other than honorable" discharge, it will be considered on a case by case basis. It depends on the circumstances and if the veteran was at fault or not. Many veterans, namely those that were drafted, were released for medical or administrative reasons that were not the result of misconduct.

VA benefits are subject to change, and only they can determine the eligibility of each veteran. If by chance you or someone that you will be making arrangements for doesn't qualify, it's better to find out now so that you can begin making other plans.

You can apply for burial in advance, though no arrangements will be planned until after the death has occurred. Approval does NOT reserve you a particular space, or guarantee any specific type of service or date of service. It just confirms that they have received and verified your information, and determined that you are eligible. You will receive a letter telling you whether you qualify or not.

A few things to consider:

- VA cemeteries do not allow graveside services.
- Services are conducted in a shelter or chapel and have a time limit. Usually thirty minutes.
- Couples share one plot, top and bottom, not side by side. Unless both spouses are veterans, then they can be buried side by side.
- The veteran information is on the front of headstone, the spouse on the back.
- You may not select your gravesite or niche. The plots are spaced in rows and your exact location will be determined by cemetery staff on the day of interment.
- There is a two year time limit in which to file a claim.

There are other restrictions, but also many other options that the cemetery staff will explain to you. Many have a scattering garden and you can have your loved ones name and dates inscribed on a brick, or stone, though their body or ashes are not present.

I have spoken with many veterans who believe that they must die first in order for their spouse to qualify, but this is not the case. If the spouse dies first, they are still eligible for burial or inurnment. There is a small fee for spouses, as of this print is $300. This could change at any time, but I assure you that this is a mere fraction of what it costs to be buried in a private cemetery.

Under very specific circumstances, dependent children may also qualify for placement in a veteran cemetery, though most don't. If you think this might apply to you or you are not sure, I strongly recommend that you contact them and find out everything you need to know. In most cases, the child must be under twenty one and have a serious disability that is documented *before* age twenty one. There are other situations that may apply. The veteran cemetery you plan on using will help you, and look into your circumstances to make a decision based on various factors.

I recently spoke with a Vietnam veteran that wants to be buried with his wife and special needs adult son. He went to the cemetery long beforehand to arrange for this, his son was approved. As with everything else I discuss in this book, don't wait until the time comes to find out.

Any rare or unusual requests will require additional planning. I have met with many veterans that changed their plans after learning about the differences between a veteran and private cemetery. I spoke with a Navy veteran who had planned on using a national veteran cemetery until he found out that he could not choose his spot. He wanted to be next to his wife, not under or above her. They purchased plots at a private cemetery even though it cost several thousand dollars.

Conversely, I have met with several people who had previously purchased plots elsewhere, but then sold them or gave them to family members so they could use the veteran cemetery. The one close to me just opened a few years ago, so I am seeing this more often.

It's not a requirement to have a military service, or to be buried in a military cemetery. It's an additional option for those who have served honorably.

Burial at Sea

This is a unique situation that requires special planning. In short, if you want this through the military, it's done only in certain places, certain times of year and because it takes place on a deployed ship, the family cannot be present.

You do not have to be a Navy or Coast Guard veteran to be buried at sea. ALL qualified veterans and their spouses can choose this option.

There are hundreds of private businesses located in coastal areas that provide this service for both burial and scattering. It's heavily regulated and laws vary from place to place. If you are considering this, (especially if you live nowhere near a coast) start researching and contacting them now as there is additional planning, permits and restrictions compared to regular ground burial.

If you would like to be present, you will want to go private. It won't be free but will be well worth it. Since I have never lived near any coastal area, I have worked with only one family who did this. Their father, a Navy veteran and avid fisherman, died in January and was cremated.

Later that summer, on his birthday, he was scattered in the ocean off the east coast. His family and friends spent the rest of the day fishing and celebrating. Don't ask me the official term but I have heard of these services being referred to as "floating funerals."

Residency Requirements

In some states, it's required that you be a resident in order to be placed in any of that state's veteran cemeteries. Other states do not have this requirement and qualified veterans and their spouses can be placed there regardless of residency. There are some differences in rules and protocol between national cemeteries and state cemeteries. The state cemeteries have the option of using state rules or national rules. Again, it is up to you to contact the cemetery you plan on using to find out all of the rules and requirements. Find out as soon as possible so that your wishes and other arrangements coincide with the cemetery requirements.

You don't want to assume anything, and then find out the hard way your loved one can't be placed in a particular location.

Private Cemeteries

For those who wish to be buried or inurned at a private cemetery, the government does not cover all of the expenses. In order to qualify for VA burial benefits in a private cemetery, you must meet the following criteria:

1. You must die from a service connected injury or illness.
2. You must die in a VA facility or a facility contracted with the VA.
3. You must be collecting, or qualified to collect a VA disability pension.

This may sound easy and that it applies to most veterans but it doesn't. There are "if's, and's, or but's" within each category and only the VA can determine who is and is not eligible. The amounts awarded under each category are a mere fraction of the actual cost in most cases. It's not something to count on.

Additionally, in many areas, funeral and cremation expenses are a separate transaction from cemetery expenses. In the places that are, it's much more convenient to take care of both at once. More often than not, funeral homes and cemeteries are not owned by the same person or company. They maintain good working relationships and are mutually dependent, but do not share or combine contracts. You must make separate arrangements at each place. I will elaborate more on this in another chapter.

I have spoken with many veterans who think that their expenses will be covered because of their rank, retirement status, time in service, combat experience, or various medals they received. These and other factors don't automatically entitle anyone to death benefits. If you don't meet the requirements, then these factors are irrelevant. Also, getting killed in an accident is not a service-connected death. You may still qualify because of other factors, but not just because the cause of death was accidental or the result of foul play.

Additionally, the VA does NOT pay for anything up front. All expenses are to be paid in advance. The receipts and paperwork (VA FORM 21-530 APPLICATION FOR BURIAL BENEFITS) are submitted. If they determine the veteran qualifies, they will pay a PARTIAL REIMBURSMENT AFTER THE FACT. I have heard of people waiting many months. One family waited over a year to receive this reimbursement. I recommend that anyone who is in charge of a veteran's estate apply for it as a variety of factors are considered. I have seen people qualify for it that I was sure would not, and vice versa.

Whether you use a veteran or private cemetery, you must first be cremated or in a casket and the VA does NOT pay for either one. I repeat, the VA DOES NOT PAY FOR WHAT HAPPENS TO YOU BEFORE YOU ARRIVE AT THE CEMETERY.

They do NOT pay for caskets, embalming, urns, cremation, flowers, folders, church or chapel services, clergy, music, receptions, etc. So many families have come into the funeral home thinking that their loved ones funeral was covered because they were a war vet.

It's emotionally and financially devastating. This belief is so widespread, that it's the very reason I began conducting seminars for veterans organizations, and private meetings for individuals and families. I too, thought this when I got out of the Army. I have countless horror stories about this that warrant their own book, but they are all very similar.

One veteran got mad at me and stomped out of a seminar when he learned this, he acted as though I had single handedly made this rule myself so I could ruin his life. Another man told me I was nuts and needed to check the facts before spreading false information. To prove me wrong, he called the VA right then during a group meeting. He got very quiet and forlorn looking when the person on the phone told him the very same thing.

One family planned an elaborate service for their father (down to the smallest detail), then announced that all we needed to do was send the bill to the VA and they will cover it. It took a while for reality to finally sink in. The funeral director nicely told the man's son again and again that it does not work that way. The poor guy turned white as a ghost. All they could afford was direct cremation with no immediate service. They should have researched this and made plans long ago.

Another family I met with had a huge blowout over this very subject several months before their father died. One of his daughters called a local veterans organization and learned about this early on. When she told her sister about it, an argument ensued and the sister hung up on her after telling her she was "as wrong as wrong can be." Fortunately, she was able to convince their father, who was dying from cancer, to make his arrangements so they could avoid family Armageddon when the time came.

This is why I feel obliged to educate and inform my fellow veterans and their families, so they can re-group and plan accordingly. Remember the 7 P's? Proper-Prior-Planning-Prevents-Piss-Poor-Performance.

Proof of Service

Whether you will be making plans for yourself or someone else, it's imperative that you gather as much information as possible. One small detail can drastically change or delay an entire situation. The most important thing of course is to have a DD-214 or other discharge document(s). Nothing will happen without this. If lost, damaged, faded or otherwise illegible, it's important to obtain a new one. Do not wait until a death has occurred, it may take some time to receive, so the sooner the better.

This also applies to any other questions or concerns you have regarding benefits and resources. Speak with someone now, if you call a VA facility you may get transferred to several people before you find the one who can help you. Persistence will pay off in the form of saving you and your family a lot of stress. It's well worth your time and a trip to the VA eligibility office. Veteran organizations and resources vary greatly from place to place so keep calling until you find the person who can help you.

In addition, keep in mind that military color or honor guards are not available in all areas. If you are on or near a military installation, or live in an area that has active veteran organizations, you will most likely be able to have them. If you live in a remote or sparsely populated area, there may or may not be anyone available to provide this service.

Beneficiaries

Another important matter that I see quite frequently with veterans is outdated wills, power of attorney, and life insurance beneficiaries. Many who made a will and/or obtained life insurance many years prior, assume that it automatically "switches over" when they get divorced.

They still have a former spouse named as the beneficiary. If they die tomorrow, their former spouse will get everything, NOT the current one. Nothing is automatic.

You must deliberately and specifically add and remove people from your will, life insurance and other accounts/assets. This is something that is supposed to be reviewed and updated periodically, especially before leaving the service, but I am surprised at how many I have met who have not taken care of this in years.

I will discuss this again in the Insurance and Legal Matters chapter. It's very important and is a major cause of devastating legal, financial, and family problems. If a veteran wants to keep a former spouse on because they share children, and add their new spouse, this must be in writing. If you have a situation such as this, or you are not sure, you will need to speak with an attorney, life insurance agent, or someone else who specializes in estate planning. Do not ignore it or think that it will magically get resolved.

In Summary

- VA burial benefits are very limited and do not cover all expenses.
- All services must be paid in advance. The VA issues a partial reimbursement afterwards. There is a two year time limit to file a claim.
- The VA does NOT directly pay for funeral or cremation services including caskets and urns.
- Military services, (especially burial at sea) require additional planning, the earlier the better.
- Obtain your DD214 and other important documents BEFORE you need them.
- Beneficiary changes are NOT automatic. You must update whenever your situation changes.
- Don't wait until a death is imminent or has already occurred. Start getting organized now.

CHAPTER 4

The Big Decision: Burial or Cremation

OF ALL THE decisions to be made, this is by far the most important. There is a world of difference between the two and both have numerous options. It's okay if you are still undecided about the smaller things such as what kinds of flowers or music you want at your service. These kinds of things can be decided later, or even at the time of service by your survivors. But the disposition of your body must be decided upon as quickly as possible after a death has occurred. It's better to decide this in advance. Of all the family squabbles I have witnessed, this has been the main reason more often than not.

Before I proceed, I will mention a few other methods of disposition. If you plan on donating your body to a medical school or other similar cause, this is something that you need to start researching and planning for now. There are numerous medical schools and other scientific research organizations that gladly accept bio-medical donations. Depending on numerous factors, not all donated bodies are accepted. Each institution has its own requirements and regulations.

This is a wonderful gift that can be used for research and educational purposes. I remember the cadaver I worked on while in mortuary school. We practiced different types of sutures. The first row looked like Frankenstein but by the 20th row, they looked very nice.

Organ Donation

Most states have an organ donation option when you obtain or renew a driver license. If your license says "ORGAN DONOR" in red letters, this is just the tip of the iceberg. It doesn't mean that your organs will be removed from your body. It's not that simple. Upon death, additional approval may be needed before a doctor or medical examiner can remove any organs.

In many cases, the decedent doesn't qualify because of various diseases, and the amount of time that has lapsed since the death occurred. It's not possible to just remove organs from one person, and put them in another. If it was, nobody would ever die. People are on transplant waiting lists for years.

Eligibility requirements and procedures vary from place to place, so if you are interested in this, I recommend asking your doctor or other medical professional. They will know where you need to go and what you need to do to begin this process.

You can also donate your body for forensic research and cadaver dog training. In most cases, you still must decide between burial or cremation, as the body is usually returned to the family for final disposition. Burial at sea also requires additional planning as it is heavily regulated with laws varying from place to place.

I touched on this in the chapter for veterans. Another more recent method is "green" cemeteries. The body is not embalmed nor placed in a casket or vault. This allows for natural decomposition. Whatever "other" options you are considering, begin researching and inquiring as soon as possible, as they require more specialized planning and coordination compared to traditional options.

The overwhelming majority of people are either cremated or buried. There are various reasons for choosing one over the other. Some people can't stand the thought of being in a box in the ground with dirt on top of them. Others see cremation as an abomination or desecration of the body. Some people cannot afford a traditional burial, others want to be scattered at sea or in the woods, etc.

I have witnessed many family disagreements over this. One

family member will say that their mother wanted a traditional burial and viewing, another will argue that when they talked to her about it a few months ago, she told them that she wanted to be cremated. If people would pre-plan, this argument would not happen. Other people just don't know because it was never discussed.

Some families are able to decide without conflict but with other families, it creates conflict.

A Short Quip on Embalming

I have spoken with many people over the years that were under the impression that embalming is mandatory, even for those who are cremated. This is not the case at all. Embalming is required for specific circumstances such as for those wishing to have a service with an open casket viewing. In this case, the body must be embalmed as quickly as possible after death occurs.

I won't elaborate on the details of decomposition, but for those who have never been near someone who has been dead for more than a few hours, suffice to say that it is not a pleasant experience. After so many hours, depending on various physiological and environmental factors, embalming is no longer an option. It's required for public viewing and in most cases when a body is to be transported.

Embalming is a surgical procedure that replaces blood and other body fluids with strong preservative chemicals that slow the rate of decomposition. It's designed to make a person look and smell nice for their funeral. It doesn't mean that the body will never decompose, but is designed as a temporary holdover until burial takes place. The blood is not "sucked" out, it is "pushed" out and replaced with chemical fluids, similar to changing the oil in a car.

Until several decades ago, it was uncommon, as most families were nearby and did not require much travel time. Most people were placed in simple wood caskets and buried shortly after their passing. Embalming is both an art and a science. I have never seen two embalmers do it the same way. Each one has their own style and formulas, and I had to re-learn at each funeral home I worked at. There are special chemicals for certain medical conditions such as jaundice and cancer. What it takes to make one person look nice can be very different for the next.

Who "Owns" the Body?

I am going to get off course for a moment to discuss a few issues regarding bodies. In a nutshell, the family "owns" the body in the sense that they get to decide on the disposition and arrangements for their loved one. They may not keep or take physical possession of them. The body is not a piece of property in the same way a television or car is. Many people have asked me if they can "just bury" someone on the farm or in the woods, the answer is no. All deaths must be reported and handled accordingly. There are strict laws regarding the handling and treatment of dead bodies.

You will find yourself in serious trouble for being in possession of, burying, or desecrating a body in any way, even if you didn't cause the death. If you own property and plan to be buried or bury someone else on it, you must designate a certain area for the sole purpose of being used as a cemetery. You may not just bury someone out in the middle of a field and then plant corn over them. It's also frowned upon to have a Viking funeral in most places.

I have been asked by many people over the years if it's mandatory to use a funeral home or cremation service. The answer is yes. You can do a lot of things on your own, or not have a service at all, but the disposition of the body must be decided. You must be buried, cremated, or donated, and it must be handled by a licensed funeral home, cremation service, or an authorized organization that accepts bio-medical donations.

In many rural areas, you can still find private family cemeteries. The laws and regulations differ from one place to another so if you are considering this, check with the appropriate agency to find out what you must do. I would start with the county, though there may be additional laws at the state level or with other agencies. It all depends on the laws, regulations, property location and other factors. If you live in town, you may not bury anyone in your yard or flower gardens.

In eras past, when someone died at home or in a rural area, it was common to bury them without notifying anyone. There may not have been anyone to notify, but that is no longer the case and hasn't been for a long time. When someone dies in a rural setting, they must be taken to a funeral home or medical examiner's office just like anyone else, depending on the circumstances.

After they are "cleared" and appropriately prepared, then they can be returned to the farm or property to be buried. I once drove an hour to pick up a 102 year old man who was born, and died at his family farm.

Several days later I drove him back for his burial in the family plot. A century ago, this would not have happened. The family would have privately buried him without any outside interference.

How Does a Death Get Reported?

Most people are "attended" when they die, meaning that their death was expected and someone is with them. Many people die in hospitals, nursing homes, hospice facilities or at home with hospice staff present. In these cases, the families don't need to do anything. The facility staff or home health attendant will notify the doctor and call whichever funeral home the family chooses. When a person is found dead unattended or unexpectedly, this is a different matter. Death's that are in any way suspicious or cause unknown are now a police/coroner matter.

During my days at the transportation service, I was called to many homes and hotel rooms after the occupant was found. Usually after family or co-workers checked on them because they did not answer their phone or show up for work. In most cases, unattended deaths are taken to the medical examiner's office for autopsy. Some are obviously, or not so obviously the result of a crime. Others die in their sleep from natural causes. *If you ever discover a deceased person, whether or not you know them, or whether or not it looks like a natural death, you need to call the police, not a funeral home.*

When an autopsy is ordered by police or a doctor, most often in the case of suspected foul play, the family is not usually charged for it. However, if a family wants an autopsy performed to find out the exact cause of death because something runs in the family, then they will have to pay for it. I worked with two families who did this and I know they both paid around $1500 for it. In addition, these private family requests are not a top priority in most cases. Police/Coroner ordered autopsies will always be done first, so your loved one may be there for a while until they have time.

Special Circumstances

In recent years, the need has arisen for special equipment and handling techniques for people who are exceptionally large. Many funeral homes now have special hoist and lifting equipment, similar to a cherry picker that you would find at an engine shop. Oversized prep room tables are available along with an array of tools and other equipment specifically designed for larger individuals. Certain places now have at least one specially designed cremation facility for this need.

If you will be making arrangements for someone with this need, find out how it will be handled before the need arises, especially if they may pass away at a private residence. Most likely, the fire department will need to be called and alternate arrangements will be made. It won't be possible for a funeral home to send out one or two people with a standard sized gurney. I have met dozens of policeman and fireman because I needed help lifting people.

Private Viewing

If you would like to have a private family viewing, this doesn't require embalming. However, when I say "family," I mean just the immediate family. As soon as other relatives and friends show up, it is no longer private, it's now public and the body must be embalmed. Before a private viewing, the body is washed and the eyes and mouth are closed. They are then covered up to the neck with a sheet.

The immediate family can spend some time with them before they are placed in a casket or prepared for cremation. Each funeral home is different and considers this on a case by case basis. In some cases, the person may not be viewable and the funeral home can refuse this service.

One family I worked with arranged for just the three of them to view their uncle before he was cremated. One of them told all their family and friends that there would be a viewing in two days at two pm. The funeral director had no choice but to refuse it. No service was planned or paid for and another family was expected at the same time.

In addition, the viewing was private for just three people. Their uncle was not embalmed. The family was upset at this one member for not listening and causing such a spectacle. If the funeral home had allowed the public viewing, they could have been closed down. Please make sure you are clear on this when making arrangements.

Viewing the Un-viewable

In some unfortunate cases, it's just not possible for a person to be viewed or to even have their closed casket present in a viewing room. I remember one family I worked with one very hot summer. Their middle-aged son died in his bed and was not discovered for nearly a week. He was in an advanced state of decomposition and there was nothing anyone could do.

When he arrived from the medical examiner's office, we immediately placed him in our refrigeration unit and then prepared to meet with his family. His extremely distraught mother just couldn't believe he was dead. She wanted to see him and was becoming increasingly irate and argumentative.

Her husband and son kept telling her that they needed to remember him the way he was, which made her even angrier. The funeral director was as nice as he could be in explaining that they needed to quickly decide between cremation and direct burial, as he needed to be removed from the funeral home as soon as possible. The arrangements were going nowhere. Her husband finally made her leave and practically had to carry her out of the building. The man's brother returned to finish making arrangements.

He opted for cremation so the family would have more time to plan a memorial service later on. This was not a good time. It never is.

If your family ever experiences something like this, please do not get angry with the funeral home staff. They are not to blame for the biological processes that occur after death. When someone is not discovered in time to be embalmed, there is nothing anyone can do. Funeral homes must consider the health and welfare of themselves and everyone who enters the building.

Funeral homes use discretion in situations like these and have the right to decide to allow for a private viewing or not. In some cases, the funeral home may allow it but require the family to sign a liability waiver. I have seen several people who were adamant about seeing their loved one even though they had been badly injured and disfigured, then wished they had not. I remember one man who viewed his brother-in-law who had been killed with an axe, right in his forehead. He nearly passed out. Another man vomited while viewing his youngest son who deliberately stepped in front of a train.

There was only one time that I can recall where the family felt at peace and got some closure after viewing their daughter. She had been missing for almost three years. Her mostly intact skeleton was found in the woods and she was identified through dental records. They still wanted a proper burial for her and selected a beautiful casket. We placed her in a private room and the family spent two hours with her before the closed casket service. I have never seen so many flowers in my life. Her family returned later that day and filled seven vehicles. They thanked us for letting them see her, and though they were devastated, it meant a lot to them to have her back for a few hours.

Restorative Art

For those who can afford it, restorative artists are available to repair and rebuild a body using various materials and techniques. This service is not available in all areas and most people don't choose it. This too is an art and there are some very talented people that can make your loved one look wonderful, despite serious injuries.

I once drove several hours in the snow to attend a seminar about this. The man was quite skilled and we spent the day looking at before, during and after photos of people that he had worked on. These services cost thousands of dollars and are usually only available in and near larger cities, some are willing to travel.

Aside from this seminar, I have seen only one family have this done. Their teenage son was killed in an accident but they were determined to have an open casket funeral. They had a restorative artist fly in from another state and paid them over $8k for six hours of work.

Back to Burial

Most people don't experience the aforementioned situations. They are attended to when they pass away, or shortly thereafter. The funeral home is called and the person is easily embalmed and prepared within a day or so of their passing. This gives the family about a week to finalize arrangements. A casket needs to be selected, along with their loved ones clothing.

For women a hairdresser is called in, this can be done by a family member or friend, but most of the time the funeral home has someone that they call when needed. They are regular hair dressers that do this in addition to their usual job at a beauty shop. Special cosmetics are used that are very different than the makeup you may have on right now. An exception is lipstick, if your loved one had a particular shade, you may bring it in and the embalmer will apply it. Many families provide a photo to help give them an idea about how they should look.

Many other things also need to be decided. Will the service be at a funeral home or church? Will the casket be open or closed? What music will be played? Will it be performed live by someone or be recorded music? Who will be officiating? Who will be the pallbearers? What kind of flowers for the casket spray? Who is writing and reading the eulogy? Who will write the obituary? Will there be a reception afterwards? Who is organizing it? Does the family want memorial donations sent to a particular charity or organization?

These and many other decisions must be made in the days following a death. It's much easier to manage when most of the details have already been planned. I have witnessed many family squabbles over seemingly minor details such as flowers, obituaries, and music, etc.

Direct Burial

Direct burial is just that. The decedent is placed in a casket and taken directly to the cemetery with no viewing or service beforehand. Embalming is not required in this case.

This option is suitable in different circumstances. Some people prefer to be buried then have a memorial service later on, or not at all. I assisted one family that was hiding from the media because their brother murdered three people before killing himself. They didn't want anyone to know where he was, so he was quickly and quietly buried with no announcement, obituary or headstone.

Another family chose this option after their mother passed away in bed. She had died over a week earlier and there was no way to have a viewing or even have her closed casket present. One of her daughters was a nurse and fully understood the condition of her mother's body. They arranged for an immediate burial and then planned to have a graveside memorial service in a few months when all of the relatives and friends could attend.

This is a viable option for those who don't plan on having a service at all, or may have one later on. I have seen many families bury their loved one with just the family, or nobody present and then head off to the church for a memorial service the same day.

In Summary

When you choose burial, whether there is to be an open casket viewing or not, you don't have much time to pull everything together. Most burials take place within about a week. As each day passes, the person may become less viewable and funeral homes charge for refrigerated storage. You don't have the option of leaving your loved one at a funeral home for an extended length of time while you decide what you want to have done. There are many decisions to be made and a lot of coordination required to put on a nice funeral in a week or less. If you are planning to be buried, then planning your service is even more important.

If the funeral homes and cemeteries are separate businesses in your area, you will have to make arrangements at both places.

CHAPTER 5

Caskets

NOW AND THEN I will hear someone use the word "coffin." The difference between a coffin and a casket is the shape. Coffins were common until recent decades. Coffins are generally mummy shaped. They are tapered at the head, wide at the shoulders, and tapered again at the feet, usually with a detached lid. They are now rarely used in North America and have been replaced with caskets, which serve the same purpose but are rectangular in shape and the lid is attached with hinges.

Some caskets are "full couch," meaning the entire lid is one piece and when open or removed, you can view the entire body. "Half-couch" means the lid is separated in the middle. Most often, the bottom, or foot end remains closed and only the upper body is viewed. In recent decades, these have become much more popular than full couch caskets.

There are many colors, styles and materials to choose from. Some funeral homes still have a casket room where you can walk through and see the real thing. Feel the lining and finish, and see all the intricate details of it, as though you would be shopping for a car or furniture. You can select the casket you want and it will be set aside for the deceased to be placed in.

Later, the funeral home will order another one to replace it. Some people prefer to shop this way but many do not for various reasons.

Seeing the caskets can cause an array of emotional reactions, and nobody wants to see the child and infant caskets. Most funeral homes do not keep an inventory of these on hand, they are usually ordered at the time of need.

Over the years, some funeral homes have removed the full caskets and used end models for display, so you can see the color and feel the material but not have the whole item in the room.

Many funeral homes have completely done away with both casket rooms and model displays, and just have a catalog to shop from. In this case, it is important to select a casket as quickly as possible because it needs to be ordered and delivered before the day of the viewing or service.

Some caskets come "as is," and others have options. Some have the option of different colored lining material, interchangeable corner brackets and handles, etc. Common corner bracket designs include flowers and crosses. While shopping, you will notice a huge difference in prices between caskets that look almost identical. The answer is in the quality of materials used. Metal caskets come in several gauges, from thin and light up to heavy and durable.

Wood caskets are made from simple pine, to oak, to cherry to mahogany. Casket linings are made of simple crepe, satin or velour with varying degrees of quality in each category. Some have more padding and thicker pillows than others. Some have adjustable inner beds that allow for the decedent to be propped up a little higher for the viewing, and then lowered back down when it's time to close the lid. Some have drawers in them to place personal items. Some have hidden, cylindrical compartments that contain the person's name and other information so they can be identified without re-opening the casket.

Some caskets have warranties. This may sound bizarre but there have been incidents of floods, earthquakes and other disasters that have un-earthed cemeteries, exposing caskets and human remains that needed to be re-buried.

Funeral homes have a special tool that opens and closes caskets.

It's pretty much an Allen wrench with a unique shape, that cannot be purchased at a hardware store.

Some caskets "seal" better than others. This is very important to many people for a variety of reasons, and can have legal ramifications in some cases. You will probably never hear a funeral director use this word when describing caskets. For regular ground burial, this isn't usually an issue and there is no way to know how it is "holding up" without exhuming someone, which is very rare.

Most often, once a person is buried, that is that. But for those who are interred above ground in a mausoleum or lawn crypt, it is very important that the casket is closed properly so as to keep the contents from leaking out. I'm not going to elaborate on this, except to say that in some cases it can discolor the outside marker and emanate a foul odor.

One day I witnessed this and spent an afternoon at a cemetery, while the crew replaced and repaired part of a mausoleum. The family complained that it was full of flies and smelled horrible. The casket had not been completely closed and the heavy marble outer plate had not been attached properly. I will stop there.

In most places, embalming is required for above ground interment. Some cemeteries require a vault that fully encases the entire casket. Other cemeteries require a simple concrete slab to be placed over the casket. This keeps the ground from sinking in and allows for easier maintenance and landscaping, but does not protect the casket from damage.

The main reason people are concerned about the casket sealing well is that they want their loved one protected from outside elements including water, mud, and insects, etc. Nobody wants to think about that. If this is a concern for you, talk to the funeral home staff and they will help you select an appropriate casket and vault.

There is no way to fully guarantee that any particular casket will never be damaged or exposed, there are too many variables that are out of anyone's control. The issue is rarely pursued in most areas.

Rental Caskets

It may sound creepy, but rental caskets are very useful in certain situations. Some people may not be physically present for their services and are not going to be buried. Some people want an open casket for their service, and then to be cremated.

The family rents a casket for the service. Then the decedent is sent to the crematory instead of a cemetery. (This is also common in cases where the body was not recovered. The family wants a casket present and places the flowers, photos and other mementos around it for the service).

Often, the price of a rental casket is not much less than purchasing a regular one. After each use, the lining is changed. You're mostly paying for the fabric padding and lining, which is then cremated with the person. This is not a popular option and most families just purchase one. I will elaborate more on this in the cremation chapter.

Custom and Specialty Caskets

Most people simply purchase a standard casket from the funeral home. However, in recent years it has become increasingly popular to design and build custom caskets. If you're planning to build one for yourself or anyone else, the first and most important step is to first go the cemetery you plan on using.

Certain specifications are required. It would be heartbreaking to spend so much time crafting a beautiful casket, only to find out it does not fit in a standard vault, or is too large for a standard sized grave plot. Additionally, a certain number, and type of handles are usually required. There are numerous other requirements.

If you are thinking about this, find out what the necessary specifications are BEFORE you build it. Each cemetery has different policies and requirements. Almost all funeral homes and cemeteries will require you to sign a waiver of liability. This releases them from any fault should something go wrong. Items purchased or made from outside sources cannot be guaranteed free of craftsmanship or material defects. What I mean to say is that if your homemade casket falls apart during the service, and your loved ones body rolls onto the floor and horrifies everyone present, you cannot file a complaint or lawsuit against the funeral home or cemetery.

Examples of Personalization

I have seen many custom caskets, and standard caskets that were modified. I remember one family I worked with, who lost their teenage son in a car accident. He was an avid fan of a local football team. Everything he owned had this team's logo on it.

His mother wanted to honor him by dressing him in his favorite jersey and covering his legs with a matching blanket. She also stated that she wished she could decorate the casket too but "something like that probably isn't possible." In fact it was.

There wouldn't be enough time to have it done professionally so the funeral director sent his wife to the mall to get a large parka with the team's colors and logos on it, along with a large sticker. She then stayed up all night cutting and sewing the emblems into his casket inlay and pillow. The sticker was placed on the casket lid. His family was as thrilled as they could be considering the circumstances.

There are many options available for customizing caskets. You can have caskets painted, detailed, or wrapped, just like a vehicle. One family purchased a plain white casket for their father a few months before he died.

They took it to their cousin's shop, removed the handles, sanded it and gave it a new paint job more befitting of their father. It had a motorcycle on the lid, with flames ripping out from under it that completely covered the top and sides. They re-assembled it and brought it back when he passed away.

Another family did something similar for a terminally ill child. They bought a little pink casket, and a relative painted the girl's favorite characters on it. She then made a custom lining and a pillow for the inside with her favorite characters and colors. They brought it back to the funeral home and we stored it for them until the time came.

When I say that there are many customization options available, I don't mean at the funeral home. I don't know of any funeral homes that can provide this service. Custom jobs are usually done at a shop or by family members. Caskets are merchandise and once you pay for, or build one, you own it whether or not there has been a death. You can have it in your home or garage, and you may paint or decorate it any way you wish.....as long as there isn't a body in it.

Years ago, I had a neighbor who proudly displayed a cremation casket in his living room. It doubled as a coffee table and as storage for extra pillows and blankets. One of my childhood friends built one in his high school's wood shop, and slept in it until his mom couldn't stand it anymore. If you plan on purchasing a casket for reasons other than a death, you will have to shop around, and more realistically, will have to make your own. Most funeral homes will not sell them to use as a prop or decoration, or any other personal use, as they do not want their name associated with something that is distasteful or unprofessional.

I have received phone calls over the years from people wanting to do this very thing. Besides, the price alone would deter most from purchasing one. It would be much easier to just make a toy version for this purpose. Casket companies only sell to licensed funeral homes, and most funeral homes only order and sell caskets to families they are serving at the time of need.

Big and Tall Caskets

I remember meeting one couple who had adopted a premature baby over 30 years prior. That little boy grew to be over seven feet tall. He had serious health problems and they knew he would not live to be very old. They knew his size would be a problem when he passed away and they needed to make special arrangements beforehand. They visited several cemeteries.

One had a "nook-and-cranny" spot that would accommodate him. It was longer than a single, standard sized plot, but not big enough for two so the cemetery sold this to them as a single plot. They then set out to find a wood worker to make his custom casket. Because this is an unusual situation, this couple was very wise in making arrangements far in advance. The outcome may not have been so favorable if they had waited until the time of need.

During a recent internet search, I discovered several businesses that specialize in custom caskets, not only in design, but in size. Most caskets are made in a standard size but some designs come in longer and/or wider sizes. In some cases, even an oversized casket will not suffice.

The business I saw online was making a special casket, the size of a double bed for a very large person. If you will be making plans for someone who falls into this category, or for someone who his unusually tall, it's important that you find out as soon as possible how this is going to be handled. You may have to purchase a second cemetery plot. Don't wait until the time comes to find out.

I have seen everything from sports team logos, hobbies, flowers, vehicles and machinery, military emblems, characters and careers. Start researching now and find out what you will need to do in order to fulfill this wish. If you cannot afford to have one shipped from one of the many companies that specialize in this fairly new field, you can approach car body shops, or anyone else who paints vehicles.

You can also have a wrap or custom decal made at just about any place that makes them. It is the same material, just obviously cut in a different shape. Either way, it's an unusual request, so you may have to contact many places before finding one who will help you. You will probably have better luck finding an individual with the artistic skills and desire to accomplish this. Be prepared to pay for it.

In Summary

The bottom line is you need to plan as far ahead as possible. The art of building and customizing caskets is just as varied and unique as any other form of art. Most people do not choose this option, and most customization projects cannot be finished on short notice. If you wait until a death has occurred, you will most likely not have time and end up just buying one from the funeral home.

Before you begin building a custom casket, make sure it meets the required specifications from the cemetery you will be placing it in.

CHAPTER 6

Cremation

IF YOU ARE planning for cremation as so many people are these days, you can relax and slow down a bit. Cremation options are very different than burial. In short, the body is placed in a concrete or brick cremation chamber or "retort" (I have heard people refer to it as an "oven" but this probably isn't the best way to think of it). They are incinerated for a few hours at a few thousand degrees.

Once completed, the skeleton is removed from the tray and placed into a machine that grinds it down to ashes. The professional term in the funeral industry is "cremated remains" or "cremains" but most people still refer to them as "ashes" so that is what I will call them.

After cremation, what remains is no longer a body, and therefore not a health hazard. The ashes are returned to the family, allowing for a wide array of options at this point. You can bury them, scatter them, keep them in your home, or have them mailed. The post office has a special label for shipping urns and ashes. Some people may find this to be distasteful, but in many cases it's the only way to return someone to their family.

For many people, it's easier to pay for a loved one's death in increments. First paying for the cremation at the time of need, later on paying for the service or celebration plans and then much later on, sometimes years, pay for the urn, niche and marker. This is one of the reasons I am so adamant about pre-planning. There is a way to pay for all of this beforehand.

Traditional Service Followed by Cremation

There is one aspect of cremation that does have a time constraint on it, and that is when someone is going to have an open casket viewing or service beforehand. I touched on this earlier while discussing burial options. In this case, the person needs to be embalmed and prepared as quickly as possible after they die, and their service planned within about a week.

The viewing or service is the same as someone who will be buried except this person will then go to the crematory instead of a cemetery. This is not the most common option for those wishing to be cremated.

Cremation Followed by Memorial Service

Another cremation option is to have a memorial service at the funeral home or another facility, usually a church. Again, the pressure is off. It can be scheduled for weeks or months after the death occurs, giving the family more time to plan for the service. In this case, the funeral home may still be involved, providing the chapel, folders, and flowers, etc. This option will cost more than a direct cremation but is worth it for those who do not want to do any of the planning themselves.

Some funeral homes have a viewing room where families can sit with their loved one. The urn is placed on a table, often with a candle or other personal touches. This is equivalent to having a regular viewing but obviously without the body present. If this is something that you would like to do, ask around to find a funeral home that provides this service. It is much more personal than just being handed your loved ones urn in an office or lobby.

Direct Cremation

This is the most popular option in many areas. You can wait any length of time to have their service, or not have one at all. Direct cremation means that the person is cremated with no plans for a service of any kind, at least not at the funeral home. This is the least expensive and easiest option. Once the ashes have been returned to the family, the funeral home is no longer needed or involved, which means that you can plan your own memorial service.

This could be anything from an organized church service to just a few people sitting at a bar sharing stories and a toast to their departed friend. Memorial services are intended to be personal and tailored to the person's life and memory.

Additionally, you can make your own folders, photo collage or memory boards, etc. You can have a DVD or slideshow made. You can get the flowers and other items on your own. Of course, you can pay a funeral home to provide these and many other items and services but if you have the time and desire, you can do it yourself. A lot of people do. And there is no hurry. You can wait weeks, months or even years before having a memorial service, or to scatter or bury them.

I remember a family that held a memorial service for their son who had died almost 15 years earlier. The estranged man had left home after high school and never came back or contacted anyone. His parents eventually hired a private investigator to track him down. They found out that he died many years ago and his ashes were in a closet at a funeral home eight states away. This family planned a full memorial service as though he had just died that day. They bought a beautiful urn, ordered flowers and folders and wrote up a nice obituary. Quite a few people attended and he was inurned in the family plot with his grand-parents.

Another family I worked with had a large reunion every three years. Their grand-parents both died in the two years since the last the reunion. They waited until the next one and incorporated the memorial service into the festivities. That way everyone could be there, as opposed to just the family in the immediate area.

The most memorable tribute I saw was for an avid bicyclist. The club he belonged to was on a long trip to the top of a mountain when he and several others were struck by a vehicle. The others lived but this young man died a few days later. A few months later, the entire club set out to finish the ride. They took turns carrying his ashes in a backpack. When they reached the top they had a wonderful memorial service and scattered his ashes next to a beautiful lake. On the way back they stopped at a resort for the buffet and wine bar. He would have loved it.

Another family that I know very well, lost their mother to cancer. She was cremated wrapped in a blanket that she got for Christmas when she was five. In one hand was her cigarette's and in the other, a giant chocolate bar. She told her kids that she absolutely did not want a funeral in any way, shape, or form. She even threatened to come back and haunt them. A few weeks later, all her friends and family gathered to celebrate her birthday. Complete with cake and balloons, a BBQ potluck, and picture boards.

The entrance table displayed her urn, a framed picture and a lit candle surrounded by flower petals and chocolate. Her daughter then kept the urn at her house for five months until what would have been her grandfather's birthday.

They buried her urn next to his, on top of his mother's casket. After the memorial tribute, her daughter pulled out a one pound chocolate bar and broke off a piece, the rest was passed around the circle. What was left was placed directly on top of the urn. Their mother would have been thrilled to have her friends stand around her, eating chocolate and sharing great memories.

Cremation Services vs Funeral Homes

I could go on for pages sharing stories of wonderful memorial services I have attended over the years, but before the cremation occurs there are a few things to consider.

There are two types of cremation services, the first one is easy. Most funeral homes and cremation services have their own crematory or contract with another firm locally. You will receive your loved ones ashes back within about a week. You have the peace of mind knowing where they are, who is caring for them, and a close estimation of when you will get them back. If you have a planned date that you will want them back for, this is the best option.

The second type is less expensive but does not offer any additional assistance. These services don't have their own crematory and may not have a contract with anyone local. They wait until they have a "full load" and then drive to another location.

If that facility doesn't have time, they drive on to another location until they can get everyone cremated. In the meantime, they keep people in refrigerated storage and you may not get your loved one back for several weeks.

I have heard from many people who felt that this is undignified. However, for some people, this is all they can afford, or they may not be in a hurry to get the ashes back, or they don't care who handles it or where it takes place. This type of service is often used for people who are unclaimed or indigent. These basic services often don't assist families with any other needs such as death certificates, etc. They strictly provide direct cremation. You are on your own for everything else. Again, no two places are alike, the quality and quantity of services varies greatly from place to place.

This is another reason I encourage people to shop around and pre-plan. You don't want to set a date for a memorial service and then find out your loved ones ashes won't be returned for several more weeks. But if this type of service suits you, and you already know how to handle all of the other necessary things that need to be settled after a death, by all means use it. You will save a few hundred dollars compared to a regular service or funeral home.

Witnessing Cremation

Another option you may consider is witnessing the cremation. Some funeral homes and cremation services have a special family room where you can witness your loved one being placed into the cremation chamber. You won't see the process itself as the heavy metal door is closed, but you can wait for the two to three hours until it is complete. Some people find this is creepy and unfathomable, but for others it provides peace of mind and closure that they were able to stay with them throughout the process.

I worked with one man who was adamant about this. He watched a show about a funeral home that was forced to close because they were caught "doubling up" and mixing several peoples ashes together, dividing them up and giving "one serving size" back to each family.

He was afraid it would happen to his mother so we arranged for a private viewing before cremating her. He stayed there the whole time. We ultimately won his trust. A few months later he came back to pre-arrange his own cremation as well as his father's.

If you would like to do this, you will need to find a funeral home that provides this service, not all of them do.

Cremation Caskets and Containers

You do not have to purchase a casket for cremation. However, you must be in a "minimum required container." Funeral homes and cremation services politely refer to it as a "rigid combustible container." It's a thick cardboard box that cost between $50 and $200 dollars. I hear a lot of grumbling about this but it's a health law, not something that funeral homes made up to get more money.

This is the least expensive option to choose. When you go to make your arrangements, you will most likely be "offered" a selection of cremation caskets to look at, if you already know about this option, you won't get duped into purchasing anything else. In fact, it is required in most places to disclose this option.

If the funeral home you plan to use allows you to bring in your own container, take advantage of it because most places don't. As with homemade caskets, the cremation container must meet certain requirements. You may not just grab and old appliance or moving box out of the garage and "call it good." In my experience, most people skip the trouble and just buy it from the funeral home.

For those wishing to have an open casket viewing or service before cremation, you can rent a casket as I discussed earlier in this chapter. You will still need to purchase the minimum required container for the actual cremation. You may also purchase an all wood casket specifically designed for cremation.

Many people find it absurd to pay hundreds of dollars for a box that is going to be completely burned up. Others are aghast at the thought of putting their loved one in a cardboard box. Only a real casket will do.

Cremation caskets are suitable for viewings and chapel services. Your loved one will remain in it instead of being removed and placed into a cardboard box. Cremation caskets and containers are not suitable for burial, as they are designed to quickly and completely incinerate. Wood burial caskets are much more durable, designed to withstand various elements and conditions over the long term.

This is something to consider as purchasing a cremation casket will add several hundred dollars to your bill. It may seem like a waste to burn it but many people feel the same way about purchasing an expensive burial casket, only to have it buried.

Urns

Once the cremation process is complete, the ashes are placed in a plastic bag, usually the twist-tie type. They are then placed in a "temporary urn" which is either a plastic or cardboard box. If you plan to scatter or keep the ashes, then you don't need to do anything else. You can purchase an urn if you would like, but it is not required unless you plan on burying in a cemetery.

If you do wish to purchase an urn, there are many styles and designs to choose from. They come in many shapes, sizes, and colors. Some are decorative, like a vase designed to be displayed on a mantle or table. Others are plain, rectangular, box shaped, round, oval etc. Others do not look like urns. I have seen some really creative and beautiful craftsmanship. There really is something for everyone.

It's not required that all of your ashes be in one container. Many people opt to have them divided up in different types of containers so that family and friends can keep a small amount.

I once worked with a family who divided up their mother's ashes into eight small, square containers so everyone had a little bit of her to keep. You may bury, scatter or keep any amount you wish.

Non-Urn Options

Many new businesses are keeping up with the cremation trend. You can have your loved ones ashes made into mini-statues, sculptures, infused into blown glass items, jewelry, and lamp shades just to name a few. Every funeral home has a catalog. Some have display rooms so you can see and feel the real thing. You can also look online for many more options.

You don't have to purchase an urn from any funeral home, and you don't have to wait until the time of need. If you find one you like and don't want to risk it being unavailable later, you can buy it now and keep it until needed. Same with having one made….death never occurs at a good time, so now is a good time.

You can also use non-urn containers. I hear people joke about using coffee cans, tackle boxes and cookie jars. I remember one family who put their dad's ashes in his old metal tool box, and put it on the shelf in his barn where he spent his life working on many projects. Another family put some of their father's ashes in an old lantern that had been in the family for almost a century. They hung it in the cabin that he spent most of his life in and scattered the rest in the lake.

Burial Urns

Specialty items and display urns are wonderful for those wishing to keep their loved ones ashes in their home, but will usually not suffice for those wishing to be buried or placed in a niche. If you plan to place an urn in a cemetery, certain types of urns and urn vaults are required. As I mentioned with homemade caskets, the first thing to do is check with the cemetery and find out what is required.

There is more wiggle room for different sized and shaped urns that will be buried as opposed to those that will be placed in a niche. It depends on the cemetery.

Recently, a family had a beautiful custom urn made for their father. They did not check with the cemetery first and the urn did not fit in the niche. They had to purchase another one that did fit. To make the best of a disappointing situation, they decided to put half of his ashes in the cemetery and keep the other half in the custom made urn.

Scattering Urns

Many designs are available for urns specifically designed for scattering. They are usually cylindrical shaped tubes. The lids are designed to open easily. Many themes are available such as patriotic, sea shore, flowers, etc. They may be used as a display urn too but are not very sturdy compared to other urns. They aren't really intended for long term use. Over the years I have sold only a few of these. Most people who intend to scatter don't see the need for one.

Scattering Laws

This is an interesting subject. I will not be able to cover every possible scenario as scattering laws vary from place to place. A variety of factors are considered and permits are required in many places. Some laws require that ashes being scattered at sea are taken a certain distance away from the shore. Other laws prohibit scattering in or near public places, in or near bodies of water, or on public lands. Scattering on private property requires permission from the owner. Check with your local municipality, usually the county though other agencies may also be involved.

The difference between scattering ashes and burying a body is obviously very different. Most people scatter in remote areas such as the woods, lakes, rivers, or family property, etc.

Very few people know about it or would even recognize what ashes look like compared to the rest of the area, especially in the woods or on a shoreline. There really is no way to enforce these laws or prove who did it, or who the ashes belonged to. I have heard several people mention the unofficial law of "don't ask, don't tell and don't get caught."

I have discovered several makeshift memorial sites while hiking in remote areas. One person scattered their dad and two brothers near a creek in a beautiful area. They left a wooden cross with a laminated poem under it. They also left a laminated note asking anyone who found this spot to please respect it and leave it untouched. Their family had camped and fished there for many decades so it was very special. The chances of anyone else knowing about this are very slim.

On the other hand, I have heard of people getting into trouble for blatantly scattering in public. One situation was at a golf course. Their dad was a lifelong golfer and they thought he would be happy at the 9th hole. Another person was caught scattering ashes in the flower bed in front of the casino their mother loved so much. Another person was caught doing the same thing outside a bingo hall.

Though it may seem like a fitting tribute to a loved one, it probably won't go as planned. I'm not sure what the penalties for doing so are, it depends on the location, circumstances and local laws. As with everything else, I recommend that you find out beforehand. Nobody wants to get arrested at, or sued over a memorial service.

In Summary

In many areas, cremation is rapidly becoming the most common form of disposition. It's much cheaper and simpler than traditional burial. By cremating, you have more time to plan for a memorial service, and decide where and when to scatter or bury the ashes.

You still need to take care of all of your other affairs. I have met with many people who felt they didn't need to worry about anything since they would "just be cremated" and not have a service. It does not save your family from other legal and financial problems if you don't pre-plan.

CHAPTER 7

Choosing the Right Funeral Home

IF YOU ALREADY know which funeral home and cemetery you will be using, this will be easy. Many families have used the same one(s) for generations and will not even consider going anywhere else. If you don't have a history with, or would like to use a different one, there are some things to consider.

No two funeral homes are alike, even the ones that have more than one location with the same name. Funeral homes are like bars. Bars all serve the same drinks, but each one has a different personality and attracts a certain clientele. Funeral homes also have a unique atmosphere.

In many small towns, there is only one. They serve everyone and have known most or all of the families in that town for generations. In larger cities, there is much more diversity and selection. Most funeral homes will serve anyone, but there are some that specialize in their own religious or ethnic group funeral rites. Whether you are Jewish, Catholic, Protestant, Greek, Buddhist or Atheist, there is at least one that will appeal to you. Some funeral homes are high-end, catering to those who can afford a more elaborate service. Others primarily serve those who want basic services, usually a direct burial or cremation with no service, or a small one with just a handful of people.

Some funeral homes are large, designed for bigger crowds and others are smaller and can only accommodate so many guests. If you decide you like a smaller one but know your service will be large, you can have this funeral home handle your arrangements but have your service held somewhere else such as a larger church or other gathering place that conducts funerals.

Traditional Services

If you want a traditional burial with a full chapel service, then you wouldn't contact a cremation service. You will want a full service funeral home. If you're planning a direct cremation with no service, then I recommend using a cremation service or a funeral home that handles a high volume of cremations.

Full service funeral homes are often much more expensive and offer the same cremation as anywhere else. Whatever you have in mind, shop around until you find the one that suits your needs and that you like. Call ahead to make sure that the person who can help you will be there, it's usually best to make an appointment so you don't disrupt a service or another family. If there are no cars in the parking lot, it's probably safe to walk in.

Location and Atmosphere

If you don't like the location, the décor or anything else, don't settle. By planning ahead, you have time to shop around and you're not under pressure to decide right away. I attended a service several years ago at a funeral home that I had never been to before. It hadn't been updated since it opened many decades earlier. You would think that for what they charge for funerals, they could afford new carpet and curtains at some point. The staff was not very friendly, not rude but very matter-of-fact business-like.

The family later told me that they had only a small selection of caskets and folders and pretty much did the same thing for all services. They only used this one because their grandmother had been long time friends with the original owner. They would not be returning. It looked like it had been quaint when it was new, but now it was in a terrible location, surrounded by development. It was very annoying to hear the outside traffic and the intercom from a nearby store during the service.

Staff

The most important thing of all is of course how the staff treats you. Are they professional yet friendly? Are they eager to sit down with you and discuss your plans? Do they adequately answer your questions? Do you feel comfortable with them? As with any other type of business, customer service is everything. A good funeral home staff will listen to your desires and concerns.

They will show you their products and services. They will recommend certain things that complement your wishes. They will be honest and tell you if what you are wanting is better purchased in a package or by itemization.

Each situation is different and one is usually better than the other. A really good funeral home will be honest if they cannot accommodate your wishes and plans. They will be respectful of your finances and avoid trying to sell you anything you cannot afford or don't want. They won't pressure you into signing a contract before you are ready to do so. Again, by planning ahead, you can spend more time looking at all of the options and will most likely be able to afford more by spreading the payments out over several years.

If you have ever purchased airline or concert tickets, you know that they are cheaper to buy in advance, and you usually get better seats. As the date approaches, the price goes up. If you wait to buy your tickets at the door, they cost even more and you are left with whatever seats are left, usually not the best ones. This same concept applies to funeral arrangements, the sooner you purchase them, the less expensive and better quality they will be. The only difference being, you are not in competition with anyone else for a limited amount of seats.

Prices

Before ANY arrangement discussion begins, the funeral home is required to give you a copy of their general price list, which is usually accompanied by the casket price list. Don't make an initial judgment based on the prices alone. The itemized prices are not the same as package prices. In addition, you will learn what is included with the prices. Some funeral homes have higher prices, and you often get what you pay for.

They may offer more comprehensive services, both before and after the service. They have more products and options to choose from, they may also have better payment plans.

Other funeral homes may have lower prices but do not offer the same level of service or as many products. Many charge interest and insurance fees. Some funeral homes do not assist families with things like death certificates or obituaries. This is why it's so important to shop around and gather as much information as possible before finalizing your arrangements.

A good funeral home will not be irritated if, after spending time with you and giving you many brochures and planning guides, you decide that another funeral home best suits your needs. They will understand that this is about you and your family and not about their sales.

House Calls

Some funeral homes will make house calls. They will come to your home and discuss arrangements and bring you relevant brochures and planning guides. This is a great service for elderly and disabled people, and people who want to make arrangements, but don't want to come to the funeral home. If you need or desire this service, call around and find out which ones are willing to do it.

One day I received a call from a young man, who knew he didn't have much time left and wanted to talk to someone. I could tell he was more depressed and lonely than wanting to plan his service. He told me that another funeral home in town had laughed at him when he asked them if they could come to him, as he was homebound.

Another funeral home never sent him the information he requested. In a January blizzard, I drove to his small apartment and sat with him for over two hours. He had no idea there was so much to think about and plan for. He was only thirty four and had two young sons. He wanted to have a nice service that they would remember.

Personal Experience

I have worked at eight funeral homes over the years, each one different from the others. One of them provided what I call "cookie cutter" funerals. It was a small town, about two thousand people, and very traditional. There was very little deviation from one service to another, very few people chose cremation or closed-casket.

A unique custom in this town was in the order of the service. Most often, open casket services take place at the front of the chapel. Those who want to can view the person before the service and again toward the end of the service. Here the open casket was in the foyer. You could not enter the chapel without viewing the person first.

When it was time to start, the casket was closed and everyone stood up and turned towards the center aisle, just like at a wedding, while the casket was wheeled to the front of the chapel. At the end of the service everyone except the family was ushered out row by row. The family had a private viewing before the casket was permanently closed. I have never seen this practice anywhere else.

One of my jobs was to post death notices around town. On a 3x5 card, I typed the person's name, date of death and where and when the service would be. Then taped them in the doorways of several popular places around town where everyone could see. Most already knew. Another unique service, this time provided by the town's people, is they would call ahead and let the funeral home know that somebody was going to pass away in the very near future. I have never seen this anywhere else. Most of the time, funeral homes learn of a death when they get the call that the person is ready to be transported.

One day while we were on the roof setting up the Christmas display, a life-long resident of the town called because she wanted to go over everything one last time before the "big day."

She heard there was a new assistant in town and wanted to meet me. We stopped what we were doing and drove out to her farm to visit for a few hours. She decided I was okay and now felt more comfortable knowing who would be embalming her. It's the strangest compliment I have ever received. She died several days later.

In small towns, the funeral director often doubles as a coach, a snowplow driver and a member of the city council. In this particular town, they appreciated a heads up whenever possible because a girls dance group and men's fly tying class used the chapel when it was available. One evening, the power was out in most of the town, so the PTA meeting was moved to the funeral home.

Another funeral home I worked at was just plain awful. One of the funeral directors was a very arrogant ego-maniac. He had no use for anyone that he deemed poor, ugly, came from an unknown family, or worse yet, anyone who had ever used the other funeral home in town. He was very rude and blunt. Being the new apprentice, I was given the families he didn't want. Long story short, the man was involved in a scandal and was practically driven out of town.

The funeral home was sold to a management company while the owner quietly retired. When I left after only four months, I found out that I was the eighth apprentice in less than two years. Most lasted about two months and a few left after only a few weeks. This is when I learned the importance of researching before relocating.

There was only one job that was easy. I worked in the office and never left to pick anyone up or to deliver death certificates. This funeral home specialized in direct cremations and small services. The phone rang off the hook. We received at least four calls a day from people requesting information. We had a steady stream of at-need business and pre-need contracts. There was no need to advertise or network, it all just flowed.

I found out about this job when I was working for a transportation service, where I picked up people from nursing homes, hospitals, and the medical examiner's office. The owner was about to retire, and I didn't know the person who was buying the business so I planned to resign. My boss told this funeral home about me and I was passed off to them. It was a welcome reprieve after lifting and loading heavy bodies over the previous year.

Corporate Owned Funeral Homes

In recent years, many funeral homes have sold themselves to large management companies. The funeral home keeps the names of its founders, such as "Smith and Jones Mortuary," but the Smith and Jones families no longer own or run it. In many cases, they are long deceased. In eras past, funeral service was a family craft passed down through generations. The funeral director and their family often lived above or next to the funeral home, similar to a church rectory. The business is no longer what it used to be and many of the younger generation have chosen to not follow their parents or grand-parents path.

Being corporate owned does not automatically mean that the funeral home is just out to get rich and "automate" the process by running as many people through as possible. This could be the intention of any funeral home.

A benefit of corporate owned funeral homes is that they are able to provide more comprehensive services and options that are often not available elsewhere. I have worked at a few of these and they are different than smaller, privately owned funeral homes. There is a difference between making arrangements for someone who has little or no family and there is not going to be a big service, and for families who do desire a larger, more detailed service. Larger funeral homes, though open to anyone, tend to cater to more of these larger families.

With the latter, you will want to choose a funeral home that provides a larger selection of caskets, urns, folders and stationary, flower options, DVD slideshows or movies, and online memorials, etc. One company I worked for makes sterling silver pendants with your loved ones thumb print on it. They also will turn a photo of your loved one into a much larger, faux canvas which is popular for memorial services.

They offered a large selection of alternate containers for ashes such as necklaces and small keepsake boxes. They made hard bound memorial books that contain photos and captions of the decedent's life. They also offered several "perks and benefits" options such as bereavement travel assistance, coverage for family members under age twenty one, survivor counseling services, travel protection and national transferability.

National Transferability

This was a very big selling point for a lot of people that I served. This is a great option for people who want to start making plans now, but know they may move to another area at some point. You can purchase your plan in your current location, then when you decide to move elsewhere, the plan will go to the nearest funeral home in that company's network in your new location. In my opinion, this alone is worth paying more for.

In addition to the funeral homes that offer this option, many life insurance policies are also honored in any location. But there are some exceptions. Whether you purchase a regular policy from a life insurance company, or a specific policy from a funeral home, make sure they offer this if it's important to you. This could create a world of problems when you pass away in another location. It doesn't mean the policy won't be honored, but there could be all kinds of red tape depending on the circumstances.

I once received a phone call from a family who had buried their father in another state. They were not aware that he had made arrangements before he moved. They planned and paid for his services at the time of need.

A few months later, while settling his affairs, they discovered that he had made prior arrangements. He never told anyone about this. Fortunately for them, his policy was revocable and they were able to cash it in. I will discuss revocability in further detail in the insurance chapter, as it can have major consequences in certain situations.

Many of these funeral homes also offer services after the service.

One I worked at had several bereavement support groups and activities for survivors. They also hold an annual candlelight memorial service in December. It's a service for anyone who has lost someone, even if they used a different funeral home. A harp player and men's quartet provided wonderful music and songs. As each name was read, a bell chimed and the family came to the front of the chapel to light a candle in memory of their loved one, then received an ornament from the Christmas tree. It's a beautiful service that I will be bringing several people to in the future. Another one had a similar service for those who had lost a pet.

If these additional options and services fit your needs and desires, then I assure you that paying higher prices is worth it. Remember, there is a difference between cost and value. Often, it is counterproductive to cut corners while trying to save a few bucks. Everyone wants to save whenever possible but understand what you may be forfeiting while doing so. Sometimes it is not worth the "extra" savings.

Let me reiterate that no two funeral homes are alike. In one place the corporate owned funeral homes and cremation services may have the highest prices, but in another town, they have the lowest prices. I have worked at and interacted with many of these funeral homes that I would definitely recommend. I have also worked at, and encountered private or family owned funeral homes that I would not recommend to anyone. It's up to you to shop around and find the one that suits you.

Happy Story

One day I met with two veterans that were both interested in direct cremation. One of them came from a large, close knit family that wouldn't have any problems taking care of everything after he died. I recommended that he go to a cremation service that cost around $900. This is less expensive but doesn't include additional services after the cremation. No problem, his family won't need them, as they have already endured several deaths in the family, and already know what to do.

The second man had very little family. His wife was an emotionally fragile woman who was easily frazzled and overwhelmed. He knew that she would need all the help she could get after he died, so I recommended a full service funeral home. It would cost about twice as much and take longer to pay off, but when the time came they would offer a much higher level of service to his wife. They will help her with his obituary, VA forms, and his death certificates, including delivering them to her home so that she does not have to come back to the funeral home.

Here are just two people with the exact same wishes, but completely different motives and needs.

Travel Protection

Another option to consider is travel protection, this may sound bizarre coming from a funeral home but it's not. I highly recommend it for anyone who travels far away from home, especially to foreign countries. You may also purchase this type of insurance through travel agencies. The difference is the travel agency coverage is often only good for a particular trip.

Some funeral homes offer a policy that requires a one-time payment that can either be paid all at once, or incorporated into a payment plan along with the rest of your funeral plans. If you pass away in another region or country, the travel expenses to get your body back home will be covered and your family will not have to pay for it, or deal with customs and travel issues. The provider specializes in handling these issues, and it's good for the rest of your life, not just for one particular trip.

If you die in another country, it's going to cost several thousand dollars to get your remains transported back home. Some countries are more cooperative than others.

Happy Story

I remember one man's family that was glad he had not only made his funeral arrangements beforehand, but also purchased this insurance. The man went on a safari trip to South America and died from a venomous spider bite. Without this coverage, it would have cost about five to six thousand dollars just to get him home. That doesn't include funeral and other expenses once returned. The insurance provider handled everything. His family would have never known what to do, or been able to pay for it.

Choosing the Right Cemetery

If you don't already know where you want to be buried, or to bury a loved one, you will need to shop around just as you would for the right funeral home. Again, in some locations, cemeteries and funeral homes are owned by the same company and you can make all of your arrangements in one contract. Though in many places, they are not, so you will have to make separate arrangements for your funeral and burial.

More Problems

Over the years, I have seen a few common misconceptions cause numerous problems. One is the idea that because one is taken care of, then all of it is. I see this often with veterans and discussed it in the veteran chapter. Because they know that they will be using a veteran cemetery free of charge, many assume that it's "all" taken care of. They don't make funeral or cremation plans because they don't think they need to.

This doesn't affect just veterans. I have met with many people who already have their plots. That's great but what about what happens before you get to the cemetery?

Horror Story

One woman I met with was thrilled when, years earlier, her parents bought a huge family plot with room for eight people. Her parents didn't purchase anything else, nor was anything else ever discussed. Many years later, when her husband became terminally ill, she called the cemetery to confirm that everything was taken care of.

They asked her what funeral home she was using. She was shocked to find out that it was not all a package deal. She went to a funeral home to make his arrangements, and had no choice but to clean out their savings to cover it.

If she would have checked into this a lot earlier, she would have had time to make payments and not be overwhelmed and shocked when the time came. When she spoke with her family, they too had not made any further plans or were even thinking about it. She was hoping to take some time off of work after her husband passed away, but now would not able to because she no longer had the savings account to fall back on.

Another family was in a similar situation. After their mother died, they came in to finalize the details. It wouldn't take long since she had made them many years earlier. When we asked them what cemetery we would be taking her to, they got very quiet. They too thought it was all a package deal and didn't even think about it. They had to quickly purchase a plot, it cost more than they were expecting and really put a damper on their plans. Again, if they had known this sooner, they could have made payments over a period of time and not been surprised.

Headstones

Headstones are also a separate purchase. You can purchase them through most cemeteries, or go straight to the monument company. They don't need to be finished by the day of the service. Many people wait until later, or never get one. A temporary marker is placed on the grave the day of burial. Some people purchase them ahead of time. Often, people will buy it after one person dies, and have most of their information inscribed on it. After they die, just the death date needs to be added.

Until the early 1970's, many of these family monuments were made with the number "19" pre inscribed on them, for the surviving spouse or other family members. Someone finally realized they should probably stop doing this, as people will live into the 2000's.

During the summer of 2000, a cemetery I was often at, filled in or removed many of these now outdated number 19's.

It's common to purchase a headstone or grave marker the same time as the plots are purchased. The difference between a headstone and a marker is that head stones are upright, and markers are flat. In some places, head stones are no longer allowed. Only flat markers as they are easy to mow over. Each cemetery is different and you will have to shop around and the find the right one, just as you would a funeral home. As with everything else discussed in this book, check into it now so you can make proper arrangements.

Grave Location

Another common situation that I have seen is when people assume they will be buried in a particular location. If you want to be placed in a location overlooking a beautiful valley, or be in the shade under a willow tree, you need to purchase it as soon as possible.

When you drive through a cemetery and see unused space, I promise you that some of it is already owned by someone else. It can also already be occupied, but no marker has been placed on it. Go to the cemetery office and find out which ones are still available and how much they cost. All graves do not cost the same.

Graves are real estate and a variety of factors determine their individual cost. If you plan to be buried, I personally recommend that you purchase your plot first. Sometimes, starting with the end and working back makes more sense. When you make your funeral plans, it will be easier knowing that you already have some place to go.

The Dreaded Salesman

When you think of sales, you probably wouldn't think about a funeral home. How do you "sell" a funeral? But that is exactly what many of them do. They sell pre-arrangements. In short, it's a life insurance policy that is specifically for funerals and cremations, that is accompanied by your specific instructions and wishes. Over the years, I have met many funeral sales people who are not unlike sales people in other businesses.

Some do a great job in explaining the products and payment plans without coming off as abrasive or overbearing. They have "the touch." Other sales people can be likened to the stereotypical used car salesman that make you want to get away as quickly as possible.

When you go to make your arrangements, I guarantee they are going to try to sell from the "top down," meaning that they are going to try to get you to purchase their most expensive products and services. Most of which are bundled into packages.

If you go in knowing you just want minimum services, they will then try to "up-sell" you by adding on little bits and pieces that, by themselves, may not seem significant but quickly add up.

Don't be surprised or offended by this, all businesses do it and they are trying to meet their sales quota. By planning ahead, you can choose the best plan that suits your needs without feeling overwhelmed or side-swiped.

I worked in sales for just seven months. I stayed as long as I did only because we had such a great team.

I loved my boss and co-workers, and knew it was going to be hard to leave. When I wrote my first resignation letter, it sounded like a "Dear John" break up letter. A few minutes before I hit the send button, I found out that another team member resigned the day before. My boss seemed quite deflated by this other person leaving, so I decided to wait awhile longer.

I enjoyed most aspects of the sales job except for the sales part. I don't sell, I educate and inform. The company I was working for taught us to SELL! SELL! SELL! It doesn't matter if our customers don't have their other legal affairs in order, or what we had to offer might not be what's best for them. Just get them to sign the contract before they go somewhere else. This didn't work for me, and I knew I was going to get fired if they found out I was sending certain veteran's over to another funeral home.

I was also not allowed to discuss the cremation and embalming process. People ask a lot of questions. Having a background in funeral service made this job difficult because I knew too much, and was not able to just focus on one aspect of the process. I wanted my clients to see the bigger picture, and to take their time processing the information, and then make the right decision.

Soon I was ready to resign again, but found out that yet another team member was leaving for another position in the company. A week later another person did the same thing. I was never going to get away! When I was finally ready to do it for the third time, I postponed again for another week because there was cake and punch at the staff meeting that afternoon.

In Summary

Remember that no two funeral homes are alike, if you don't already know which one you plan on using, you will need to shop around. Find out what services and options they offer, what kind of payment plans are available, etc. Ask trusted friends what funeral homes their family has used.

Most funeral homes have websites that explain many of the issues that you may be considering so you can get started before making a trip. Some have a downloadable planning guide that you can write in.

As you are thinking about what you want for your service, make a list of questions and concerns. Make sure you have chosen the right funeral home and cemetery, the right services and products, and have a clear understanding of everything before you sign a contract.

Pre-planning can help you avoid many surprises, overspending, or leaving inadequate plans and funds. The funeral home and cemetery that you choose will walk you through their process and explain everything in more detail. Remember that in many places these are separate transactions and you have to take care of both individually.

By going in at least somewhat informed, the planning process will be much easier. Don't feel pressured. You don't have to purchase anything on your first visit. If you wait until the time of need, this process is eliminated and you don't have time to plan ahead. Most people in this situation end up panicking and overspending, and then later wondering if they did the right thing. By pre-planning, you eliminate this burden.

This is about you and your family, and you have every right to interview different funeral homes and shop around before making a decision.

CHAPTER 8

Insurance and Legal Matters

AS I BEGAN this chapter, I intended to separate the two subjects of insurance and legal matters, but this is where things can start getting complicated, and to overlap each other. Your estate is a pie, made up of several smaller pieces. Some of the pieces can stand alone and be handled individually but other pieces cannot. One small detail can change the outcome of the rest of the pie.

I have seen many cases where someone planned their funeral down to the last detail, but did not take care of something else properly, and their family still ended up in court. Conversely, I have also seen cases where someone planned out their estate and left equal shares to all of their beneficiaries, but left out funeral instructions and their family still got into a big fight over how that would be handled.

As you get your affairs in order, make sure that ALL of them get handled, and they are all compatible. You don't want to leave loose ends that create new problems. Your insurance policies, funeral plans, real estate, debts/liabilities, assets/holdings, power of attorney, last will and testament, advance directives and your family circumstances and dynamics are all connected to each other.

I strongly recommend having as many of your affairs as possible handled by as few people as possible. It really helps to have one attorney, one insurance agent and one executor/executrix handling your affairs. The more fingers that are in the pot, the more problems, hold ups and additional expenses are possible.

Life Insurance

In the early days, it was called "death insurance," meaning that after you died, your beneficiaries collected on the policy to replace your income until they get back on their feet. At some point it was changed to "life insurance." Call it whatever you want, both are correct and serve the same purpose.

This is a complicated issue that has countless variables for countless scenarios. I will explain certain aspects of it as it pertains to final arrangements. In some cases, having life insurance simply provides a false sense of security. Having it doesn't mean that your survivor's will be okay and all of your debts and expenses will be covered.

Life insurance laws and policy types vary greatly from state to state and from one company to another. I am not going to discuss the differences between whole or term policies, premium calculations or other topics that you should discuss with your insurance agent.

Everyone is different so it's up to you and your agent to determine the best type of policy to suit your needs. Some policies provide pretty straightforward coverage, if you die tomorrow your beneficiaries get the money and that is that. It sounds pretty easy but there are differences in policies and amounts that can have a big impact when it is time to pay for a funeral.

I have seen several common issues persist over the years that have caused great heartache for families after the death of a loved one.

How Fast Does It Pay?

I have met with many people over the years who felt no need to pre-plan in any way because they had "great" life insurance. Let's take a closer look at this. They may have had a "great" amount of coverage but in many cases, the insurance did not pay out for several weeks. The family had to come up with other funds while they were waiting to receive it.

Many families used credit cards. Some families had to get bank loans and use other assets as collateral.

Other families were able to borrow the money from relatives. In these situations, they were fortunate to have other resources to pay for their loved ones funerals. Some funeral homes will allow people to pay after they receive these funds, depending on state laws, the funeral home, conditions of policy and the overall estate of the decedent.

I have seen this most often in smaller towns where the funeral directors have known the family for many years, and they also know the insurance agent and attorney handling the deceased person's estate. One small town funeral home I worked at, directly and privately financed funerals for several families that they had known for generations. Don't count on this anywhere else. More often than not, all services must be paid for up front.

Other families did not fare so well. I saw many over the years, who had to drastically alter their plans because immediate funds were not available. One family in particular ended up opting for a direct cremation because they had no other resources. The life insurance check would not arrive for at least thirty days, possibly longer. If it had paid out sooner, or they had other funds, they could have had the more elaborate service they were wanting.

Some families had to have their loved one sent to another funeral home that would work with them. Most funeral homes charge for sending someone to, or receiving them from another funeral home.

If you have ever negotiated a settlement with any insurance company or court, you know all too well that everything usually ended up costing much more, and took longer than you expected. When the check finally arrived, you couldn't use it for what you had intended because you had to go back and pay for all of the expenses that accrued while you were waiting.

How Much Is Enough?

A "lot" of money looks like a lot of money when you don't have it, but when it's time to pay off debts and settle an estate, it can quickly become very little or not enough. Especially for those who die from an injury or illness that results in large medical expenses, in addition to all of the other bills and debts.

For example, let's say you have a life insurance policy for $50,000. You die tomorrow and leave behind $200,000 in bills. Now what for your survivors? How will they pay for the other $150, 000 after losing your income? The $50k may cover your funeral expenses and some living expenses for a while but won't cover the other debts. Do you have mortgage insurance or will they have to sell the house? Will your spouse be able to continue the car payments? Will your spouse's income be enough to live on and for how long? What about your children's college funds? What about your family's emergency savings fund?

If you're younger and have a family to support, then life insurance is probably necessary. Your family will need to replace your lost income. Please do not blow this off and think that it won't happen to you. If you have never experienced an unexpected or tragic death in your family, I assure you that it's a very unpleasant experience. It can turn your life upside down and open up a very messy can of worms.

For the past few years, I have been bugging one of my friends to get life insurance. He has a wife and three small children. If he dies tomorrow, they will have nothing. If she dies tomorrow, then he will be a single dad and have to completely re-arrange his life and cut his work hours or not work at all. If they both die simultaneously, who will raise their kids? Now what?

Horror Story

I know a young woman who made a really bad decision that she soon paid dearly for. When she got married, they bought life insurance policies for $350k each. The monthly premium was only about $30 for both of them. They had great jobs, but when they learned they were pregnant with triplets, they decided that it would be best for her to stay home.

They made numerous adjustments to prepare for the big change, especially the loss of her income. They refinanced their house, then sold their jet skis and time share condo. They also cut some other, smaller corners and one of them was their life insurance. After all, they were young and healthy, and he had a free policy through his employer.

You already know where this story is going. A few years later he died unexpectedly. His policy through work was just enough to pay for his funeral and burial expenses and some of their smaller bills. The social security benefits she received were not enough to live on, so in addition to losing her husband, she also lost the house and everything in it. She had no choice but to return home and live with her parents.

Imagine how different the outcome would have been if they had kept their policies current. A few years later, she re-married and this time had large, iron-clad policies on herself and her new husband. She is one of countless people who learn the hard way how important it is to be prepared. The worst mistake anyone can make is to think that something bad could never happen to them or their family.

Overall, life insurance is great when you are young, healthy and working. As the years go by, life changes and therefore needs change. You may need more coverage when your thirty five and have a mortgage and a family to support. Years later, the kids are grown, the house is paid off and you're looking at retirement.

You no longer need the same coverage you did back then. As you get older and/or start having health issues, the policy amounts either stay the same, or more often, decrease while the premiums increase. In some situations, you can't get it at all.

I have seen many people pay into policies for years with the intent of having it go towards their final expenses when they die. More often than not, this is not the best plan. As I mentioned earlier, the cost of funerals and cremations will continue to rise, so if you are paying for a policy over the long term, you may as well specifically pre-plan and pay for your funeral expenses. When you look at how much you have paid in premiums compared to inflation, you have lost a lot more than just the premium amount. You have lost the significant savings of yesteryear's prices, and could have had it all paid for by now.

If you know that you have adequate coverage and other assets that will provide for your family, that's great. If you know that your family will cooperate and agree on not only what kind of funeral you should have, but all the other estate matters and there won't be any fighting or legal problems, that's great too. You are the minority. But the reality for most people is there will be problems and issues. Many could be prevented with prior planning and preparation.

Even if you are wealthy, it's still a good idea to plan your funeral or cremation services. Having lots of money does not prevent family fights, or difficulty in decision making abilities. Every family reacts differently. I cannot count how many people I have encountered who believe that having lots of money automatically avoids problems. Quite often it has the opposite effect.

Other Predicaments

I have a close friend that realized he needed to get his legal affairs in order after his father died. If anything had happened to him while his dad was alive, it wouldn't have been a problem. His dad would have been able to handle it, but now he had to change everything and appoint a new power of attorney. He is single with no children and aside from some scattered cousins, the only blood family left was his older brother.

His brother was in an accident years earlier, resulting in significant brain damage. He would never be able to handle any legal affairs or make any sound decisions. He understood that if something happened to him, his disabled brother would be considered his next of kin, both biologically and legally. He had no choice but to legally disown him.

He provided for him and listed all the items that he wanted his brother to have, but gave all power and decision making rights to his pastor. He wasn't really concerned about what would happen if he died, but was very concerned about what would happen if he became incapacitated. He was very honest and realistic about his situation and then took the right action to resolve it. If you have a similar situation, you will need to plan accordingly.

Happy Story

Recently, I met with a neighbor that asked me about "all of this funeral stuff." She was confused and had many questions. Many years had passed since she and her late husband had planned anything. They purchased their burial plots and headstones shortly after they married in the early 1950's, but they did not make funeral plans. When he passed away many years ago, she had enough in savings to cover it, but never made any plans for herself. She thought about it many times but assumed her life insurance policy would cover everything.

She brought me all of her paperwork and we spent the afternoon going through it. The first problem was that her husband had qualified for veteran benefits, but she didn't know anything about them so she never applied. It was too late now, too many years had passed. In addition, she had been paying on a small life insurance policy for many years. It was only about five dollars a month to start. That seems inexpensive, but since then the price of funerals had gone up significantly, in addition to the premiums.

Five dollars a month became twelve for the same amount of coverage. If she were to die now, the policy would barely cover a basic service. It would have covered much more if she had died many years ago. We calculated that she had paid nearly $900 in premiums over the years. She would have been better off purchasing a specific policy at a funeral home. It would have been paid off by now and she would have a much nicer service at yesteryear's prices. She decided to cut her losses and cancel the policy. Fortunately, she had no debt, and received her husband's pension and enough social security to live on.

Her legal affairs were also outdated, everything still had her husband's name on them so I encouraged her to contact an attorney and update her will and power of attorney. When they last made one, their grand kids were still small. Now they were all adults.

A week later, I took her to the funeral home and she signed a contract, to pay about $100 per month for five years. She now felt very relieved to have this burden lifted. When she told her family what she had done, one of her son's sent her enough money to pay off the contract early.

Horror Story

Another person I worked with did not fare so well. This woman was in her mid-thirties and had taken care of her mother the last several years. She lived with her mother and did not work outside the home. She was sure that her mother's $50,000 life insurance policy would cover everything until she got back on her feet. When her mother retired, one of the benefits was continued life insurance. That sounds nice, except that someone either didn't mention, or she misunderstood, and overlooked the fact that the amount diminished after retirement. $50k became $15k, if she wanted to keep the $50k, she would have to start paying for it, and the premiums would be higher than when she was working.

In the years since retirement, she did not update or check into anything. She just assumed her daughter would be able to take care of everything since she lived with her. She did not put her daughter on her checking account or sign her car title over to her. She had no will or power of attorney.

This young woman ended up in a mess after her mother died. She was able to pay for her cremation but had to go to court to settle all of the other matters. She found out the hard way that her mother was behind on property taxes and some other bills. She had to sell her mother's house. It took several months for her to gain access to her mother's accounts and get the car title. If her mom would have just done this beforehand, it would have been a simple case closed.

Another Horror Story

Another family was visited by the karma fairy. The patriarch of the family was in very poor health and things were not looking good. He and his first wife divorced after their youngest finished college. When he re-married, there was non-stop strife between his children and his new wife. As is so common, this man did not update his legal affairs to fit the new circumstances. He eventually ended up in the hospital with a life threatening condition.

When his death appeared imminent, his kids told his wife that she needed to get out of "their" house. They also began putting things up for sale and removing items from his home. As fate would have it, the man stabilized and temporarily recovered. When he found out what they had done, he completely and permanently disowned and cut them out of his life and will. When he died several months later, his wife got every last penny.

The Worst Horror Story

The worst situation I ever saw involved a man that died in a car accident. He was highly successful. He always told his siblings that they would inherit everything since he had no plans to marry or have children. They made big funeral plans, a full traditional burial with a public viewing at a large church that would accommodate hundreds of people. They also purchased a very large headstone. They paid for everything themselves since they would be reimbursed from his estate.

Two days after the funeral, they were contacted by his attorney. Right before his death, he was about to be indicted on major charges including fraud and embezzlement. All of his assets and accounts were seized. As the investigation continued, it became apparent that the accident was looking more like a suicide. This man's entire life was phony. He had been involved with some shady characters and made a career out of scheming, plotting and covering up all of his fake businesses and accounts.

His activities went much deeper than anyone could imagine and every time they thought it was over, or couldn't get any worse, some-thing else would surface. His family was also investigated because they were named beneficiaries and therefore possibly involved. They went through the wringer just to recover personal family items that had no monetary value. Things like photo albums and his college trophy collection. They were not allowed in his home or office, and never received a dime.

Though they eventually recovered these items and were cleared of any involvement, it left permanent emotional scars on them. Needless to say, this family was devastated, not only from his death, but from all the publicity and legal problems. The worst part was all the years of elaborate deceit.

Happy Story

Several years ago, I received a call from one of my army buddies. His parents had taken care of all these matters while he was still serving overseas. They had named his older sister as power of attorney, and executrix of their estate. Eventually, she developed Alzheimer's disease in her late fifties, and was no longer able to make any decisions. As soon as he returned, they contacted the law firm that had prepared all of their paperwork several years prior.

They learned that the attorney they had worked with was disbarred, and in prison for forgery and fraud. Though they were sure that none of their matters were affected by this man's actions, they decided to have it all re-done with another attorney. They paid for it, but felt it was well worth it to ensure that there would be no surprises or problems later on. They also made funeral plans for his sister. Good move.

More Problems

Many seemingly simple things are often overlooked or never even thought about. Many people are innocently ignorant until an unpleasant reality presents itself. One of those things is the subject of "kin" or "family."

Many states have laws that prevent people from completely disowning, or withholding assets from a spouse. However, in many places and cases, "next-of-kin" is your children first, not your spouse.

Each state is different and there are numerous factors that determine the outcome of this type of situation.

Having one of your adult children live with you does not mean they will get everything after you die, even if you want them to. Living with someone, whether a romantic partner or roommate/friend for many years does not automatically mean they will get everything, even if you want them to. Telling your sister that you want her to have your silver and china collection will not guarantee that she will get it.

I have some friends who live with their oldest daughter. They are estranged from their two other children because of drug issues. They were under the impression that the daughter they lived with would handle everything and get everything after they die. If it's not in writing, it doesn't exist. They learned that they needed to do a will and specifically name her as their sole beneficiary, guardian and executrix of their estate. They also needed to add her to their bank accounts. Otherwise, their estate would go to probate and other family members could intervene.

Probate

I do not wish probate on my worst enemy. When you die without leaving a will, it is called "intestate." Meaning you died without leaving any instructions or naming any beneficiaries. In a nutshell, the state decides how your estate will be settled and who gets what. Uncle Sam usually comes first. If you owe any kind of taxes, they are paid first. Then they look at your other debts and legal matters, and go down the list. In some places, the funeral home is paid first.

Long story short, there may not be anything left for the people that you want it to go to. Depending on various factors, probate can stretch on for months or even years.

If you are really lucky, it may take only 4-6 months, if you are moderately lucky, it can take about a year. Otherwise, it usually takes well over a year, often longer depending on the circumstances, and it rarely works out in your beneficiaries favor.

Regardless of your situation, you need to specifically decide how you want your estate to be settled. You don't have to be wealthy or have a vast estate in order to have a problem. Be honest with yourself about your family and financial situation.

If you don't make these decisions beforehand, someone else will make them and it may not be what you had planned. When I did my own Last Will and Testament, I specifically stated who my "family" is and who gets what. Should anyone else try to claim me or contest my wishes, I have left them ten dollars. This will come in handy when I win the lottery, then die two days later and a bunch of long lost relatives show up.

Beneficiaries

No matter what type of policies you have, or how you have your estate arranged, make sure you correctly name your beneficiaries. As I mentioned earlier, you must keep everything updated. A common mistake is assuming that because you got divorced, then re-married, that your current spouse is automatically entitled.

Anytime there has been a change in your situation you need to specifically add and remove people. I have seen this with many veterans over the years. Years earlier, they named their former spouse on their life insurance and/or their will. They never changed it and if they die tomorrow, the former spouse will get it, NOT the current one.

I have spoken with a few people who successfully contested this. Some places have time limit laws that will allow for this situation, but why risk it? If you have a new spouse, and especially if you have children with the new spouse, it's not worth the risk. It's much faster, easier and cheaper to just update it.

You need to update in the event of a death, divorce, marriage, birth, adoption, disability, estrangement, a child becomes an adult, etc. Other things to consider when estate planning: Do you have business partners? Do you serve on any boards or councils? Do you own property or time shares? Have you co-signed anything? Are any of your beneficiaries in prison? Are any of your beneficiaries mentally disabled? Do you have children from different marriages? Are any of them still underage? Do you have unresolved debts or other legal matters with a former spouse? Does your new spouse also have children from prior marriages?

Are you now living in another state that has different laws pertaining to community property, common law marriage, and who is considered next of kin? Has there been a significant change in your financial status? Are any of your beneficiaries having legal problems, such as being sued or garnished? Don't assume anything or think that everything will somehow work itself out, because it won't.

Additionally, if you have any family members that are dishonest, unreliable, irresponsible, or will in any other way cause problems, then you will need to plan accordingly. You will want to protect the ones you do want to inherit your assets from anyone else that you don't. Stay informed of any changes in your life, AND theirs that will cause any adverse effects on your wishes and beneficiaries.

Traditionally, the oldest child, namely the son, was left in charge of family affairs. This is not always the best situation. You will want to choose a family member that is able and willing to handle your affairs. What if you and your spouse or other family members die at the same time? Now who is in charge of your affairs? As with everything else, plan B is usually needed.

A Close Call Happy Story

Years ago, I met with a woman who got all of her affairs updated just in time. I first met her when her dad died, and again two months later when her mom died. She has three adult children. Two were responsible, but her oldest son had unfortunately lost his way in life. He was in and out of jail, owed back taxes, back child support, numerous fines, legal fees and restitution from his many squabbles with the law.

Her lawyer advised her that if she left him in charge of her estate, or any money, there was a good chance there would be some serious government interference that could possibly cause major holdups and hassles for her other two children. The thought of her other two kids having to go to court, and her money going towards legal messes scared her into updating everything.

She received several second and third hand inheritances over the years, including land. She was about to retire after 46 years at the same company, had not removed her late husband from any documents, titles and policies, and still had property deeds in her parents and grandparents names. This attorney found all kinds of loose ends, and glitches that could be disastrous for her family, including an obscure but important technicality in one of her upcoming retirement funds. She got it fixed just weeks before announcing her retirement.

I pretty much forgot about her, until several months later when her daughter called the funeral home and asked if we still carried the same casket that they had purchased for the grandparents a year earlier. Their mother was on her death bed, and wanted to be in the same model and color casket as her parents, and we should be expecting the call any day now....it came that night.

When they came in to make arrangements, they informed us that their aunt and uncle were both in a hospice facility, and we would soon be getting those calls too. This family's situation is not all that uncommon. I have experienced this in my family also, where not just one or two, but several people die within a short amount of time of each other. Thankfully, they were spared from all of the legal messes that they would have had if their mom had not updated everything, just months before her passing.

More Things to Consider

Remember that whoever is responsible for settling your estate after you die will be spending a lot of time doing so. They may be missing work and other obligations, especially if they have to go to court for any reason. Most people appoint a secondary person to handle their estate if the primary person is not able to. Make sure that the person(s) you select are both willing AND capable. Many are one or the other but not both.

This may not be as easy as it sounds. When I was preparing my will and other legal matters, I started thinking about all the wonderful cousins I have. I adore them, and wish we could see each other more often and not just at funerals. If something happened to me tomorrow, I know they would be devastated and WANT to help. But they are scattered over several states and Canada.

They have kids, grandkids, and jobs. Several are disabled and unable to travel or handle any kind legal matters. What if something happened to them? Would I be able to drop everything and get there, and then settle their estate? The answer is no. It took me awhile to find the right person that I know can handle everything, both timely and correctly.

Another Dilemma

I've seen many situations where family members died together. One woman had only one daughter and she was in charge of all of her affairs. They both died together in a car wreck on Valentine's Day. Her estate went into probate because she had not named a second-ary person in any of her documents. I have also seen several incidents where spouses died together.

More Surprises

After my mother died, it took three weeks to get her apartment cleared out. I had to return all of her cable boxes and equipment. The man at the cable company informed me that I was not on her account and therefore not authorized to make any changes. I said "she died, would you like to call her?" He started arguing with me....I told him to have a nice day and walked out.

I had to have the utilities turned off and pay the final bill. When I closed her bank accounts, they "allowed" me to pay off her credit card but not close it. They were charging her $15 a month to have a zero balance. After several months of annoying phone calls, I told them that I'm sure she isn't concerned about her credit rating at this point. I never heard from them again.

I had to have someone follow me to my place in her car, and then drive them back. I had to get the title changed to my name, and get a new insurance policy since I had been on hers for several years.

She made a list of things she wanted her friends and family to have. A very heavy china hutch had to be delivered to the home of a cousin who is wheelchair bound, which required re-arranging part of their house. Many items had to be delivered to various homes around town. Fortunately, I had access to two men with a truck.

After all the friends and family got what they wanted, we made several trips to a thrift store, and my minimally furnished apartment was then stacked to the ceiling. My mom had a lot of stuff because some of it was her mother's and aunt's belongings. They both died shortly before she did, and she was still going through it when she learned that she was terminally ill.

This was pretty easy, she started giving things away before she died, and since she had all of her affairs in order, I didn't have to go to court or pay for any attorney services. For people who have to settle the estate of someone who did not pre-plan, the list of things to do can be endless, and take many months or even years to complete. It's a big commitment so make sure you have the right person handling it.

Transfer on Death Deed

Some states (about half of them) allow real estate deeds to be passed to your beneficiaries while you are still alive. The transfer won't be complete until after your death, but may keep your beneficiaries out of probate. There are numerous factors and conditions involved with this transaction so you will need to check with your state and your attorney. This does not replace a will, or instructions for other matters though. All other matters still need to be settled. For residents of the states that provide this, it is a wonderful way to eliminate yet another obstacle and make things easier to deal with after your passing.

Back to Insurance

There are insurance companies out there that sell general policies, and some that sell policies that are strictly for final expenses but they are not affiliated with any particular funeral home or cemetery. If these policies work for you, then by all means take advantage of them. Make sure you understand them, and find out how quickly they will pay out at the time of need.

A downfall to some of these policies is that they are not inflation proof. You purchase a policy for a certain amount and it stays the same. Decades later, the cost of funeral and cremations has risen significantly and what was a "big" policy 30 years ago is now very small, and possibly not enough to cover the type of service you desire. Again, make sure you understand everything before you purchase any policy.

Personally, I recommend going straight to the funeral home that you intend to use. It's much easier to use their company, who has specifically tailored their policies to the funeral homes and cemeteries in their network. This way you cut out a middle man that may, or may not be easy to deal with when it's time to collect.

There are other benefits to purchasing directly from a funeral home. One being that you lock in today's price. What costs $5k today will easily cost $20k in a few decades. Purchase it today, and when the time comes several decades later, and the price has gone up exponentially, your survivor's will not have to pay the inflated difference.

Another benefit is that you won't have to worry about how fast it will pay out, the funeral home will put in the claim and you don't have to deal with any of it, or worry about having to pay for it in the meantime. This isn't always the case with regular life insurance policies.

If the funeral home you want to use doesn't offer these benefits, or a feasible payment plan, you may want to find another one that does. The whole point of pre-arranging is to avoid as many pitfalls and surprises as possible, and to make things as easy as possible for your survivor's.

When you sign a pre-need contract with a funeral home and/ or cemetery, your decisions are officially recorded and the contract becomes a legally binding document. This brings me to the next very important matter. Before your contract is finalized, you will be asked to choose between revocable and irrevocable.

Revocable vs. Irrevocable

Just two tiny letters "i" and "r" can make a world of difference. There are pros and cons to both. The funeral home will explain it, but cannot decide for you. Revocable means that you can change your mind later and either cash in the policy, or make changes to your original decisions. Irrevocable means that it's ironclad and cannot be cashed in.

Revocable contracts are good for people who know that they want to start their plans now but may change their mind later. I met with a man who had arranged for a direct cremation many years earlier. He was a confirmed bachelor and didn't have many family or friends who would attend his service. Many years later, he finally met someone and got married.

He inherited a new family and became Papa to an army of kids, grand-kids, nieces and nephews. He realized that when he died, there would be a service and he wanted to plan a nice one that they would remember. So he cancelled his cremation plans and upgraded to a traditional burial.

One day while I was looking through old pre-need files, one caught my eye because the purchaser was just two weeks younger than me. I read through it and was surprised that a nineteen year old would be making funeral plans.

Her file was detailed but had not been updated in over twenty years, so I called the insurance company to see if the account was still active. It was, and had grown quite a bit. They told me that their last contact with this woman was about twelve years ago. I knew there was a good chance she had a different last name.

After some rainy afternoon detective work, I found her parents. She was glad I contacted her and told me that when she got divorced and moved, she never heard from the insurance company again. She thought she had been scammed, so she cut the loss and never pursued it. She came in and updated everything and made her policy irrevocable. The next step was to bring her new husband in and plan for his. She had planned her funeral so young because her family had three deaths in five months. I can relate to that.

Another woman planned a traditional burial twenty five years earlier, but changed her mind in recent months, after the last of her siblings died.

Almost everyone she knew had already passed away, or moved away and there would probably be only a few people attending. She decided there was no need for the open casket viewing. She cashed in her policy and purchased a basic cremation package. Having a revocable contract worked out for these people but it can have the opposite affect for others.

Horror Story

A woman pre-arranged her traditional burial many years ago after her husband died. I don't know if she deliberately opted for revocable or if she didn't understand it. As the years went by, most of her family passed away. She had one grandson, who lived with her and was supposedly taking care of her. As her dementia worsened, he convinced her to let him legally control her affairs. He sold all of her property, her house, and cashed in her funeral policy to feed his drug addiction.

He ended up back in jail and she went to a nursing home. When she died, there was no money for a funeral. She was cremated, and her ashes left in a cardboard box at the funeral home, unclaimed, for several years. Her grandson eventually paid the bill and had her urn buried in what should have been her burial plot. If her contract had been irrevocable, he would not have been able to touch it and she would have had her traditional service.

Revocable is a bad choice for anyone who will go to a nursing home or other facility on government assistance. The government will claim it as an asset and cash it in. It can also be a bad choice if you have any untrustworthy family members.

Irrevocable

Nobody can touch it, period. This includes the government and unscrupulous family members. If there is any chance at all that either situation may apply to you, make sure that you know what you want and won't change your mind. Then make it irrevocable. I received many phone calls from social workers, state agencies and family members asking about people's policy status. Many sounded dismayed when they learned that they could not touch it.

In some cases, it can turn out to not be the best decision. I worked with one family that was not aware that their mother had made arrangements a few years prior. The payments were automatically taken from her checking account, which she was no longer aware of. Her dementia was progressing so they were selling her home, and making other changes in preparation for her move to an assisted living facility.

When they found the funeral contract and asked her about it, she didn't remember ever making such plans. She had inadvertently gone to a different funeral home than the one they used for her husband and other family members. Her kids contacted the funeral home, and indeed, the contract was irrevocable. There was no way to change it or cash it in. They decided to cut the loss and stopped the payments. When she died, they went to their preferred funeral home and paid for other arrangements.

The only way to really get out of an irrevocable contract is to stop the payments, accept the loss, and make other arrangements somewhere else. However, this plan won't work in all situations.

When you're ready to make your arrangements, make sure you understand this and that the choice you make fits your situation. This is another of the many reasons I want people to get educated and plan ahead. Find out everything you need to know before signing the contract.

In Summary

I invite you to talk to any attorney, estate/financial planner, life insurance agent, funeral director or even a social worker that works with the elderly. I promise that they too, could spend hours telling you horror stories about what happens to families when someone dies without making any arrangements or leaving adequate instructions. They can also tell you that the primary source of estate fraud and theft is family.

Don't wait until there is a problem, not just a death, but any problem. Your "family" that you have not seen in years may have legal priority over the love of your life, who you have lived with for many years and would want everything to go to.

Please do not assume that because you have life insurance, that your family is safe and everything will be okay. Don't assume anything. Life insurance is one of those things that you don't need until you need it. Then when you need it and don't have it, there is now a major problem. Many people make the mistake of having just enough to cover their debts or final expenses, but not enough for their survivor's to live on until they get re-settled.

I strongly recommend purchasing a policy specifically for your final expenses, separate from, and in addition to your regular life insurance policies. Conserve your other insurance for your family's more immediate, tangible needs.

All kinds of sticky situations can result from a seemingly minor detail. Start getting your affairs in order now. It's not an event, it's a process. It can take time to determine what issues you have and how you want your estate handled and for what kind of funeral or memorial service you want, and to figure out how you're going to pay for it.

It's understandable if you don't know what kind of service you want right now, or your top priority is getting the house paid off, or all of your children through college. I don't mean to imply that you need to hurry up because you might die tomorrow. There is a good chance you won't, or even next week or next year. But there is always that "what if" cloud hovering overhead.

At least start thinking about it, start checking into it if you haven't already. Make it a goal to get your arrangements paid for as soon as possible. You will be glad you did and your family will be glad too. It's a huge burden and expense to remove from your already full plate. It's hard enough to deal with the loss of a loved one. Having additional financial and family problems makes it even harder.

CHAPTER 9

Basic Planning

I'M ASSUMING THAT everyone reading this has, at some point, made plans for a life event of some sort. It could be a short, temporary event such as a weekend getaway or spa retreat. Other events are far off in the future such as sending a child to college, retiring or getting your mortgage paid off. These events are planned for as far in advance as possible. You know the day is coming, but not right now. You have other things to take care of and you want to enjoy your life now and take it one step at a time. This is understandable and normal.

Think about a big vacation you and your family went on. There were many things to plan out and purchase such as plane tickets, how much luggage, how many days/nights, coordinating transportation from the airport to a hotel, and what attractions or destinations you planned to visit. If you drove, you most likely had your car serviced before you left, made sure your insurance and roadside assistance was up to date, then calculated the mileage and fuel costs, etc.

In either case, you probably started packing several days before the trip. Additionally, you probably also arranged to stop the newspaper, the mail, and leave your pets with someone, or have someone house and pet sit for you. You had to get the time off from work, and arrange all of your other appointments and obligations around your vacation dates. You made sure that family and neighbors knew where you were going, how they could reach you and when you would be back.

In any event, you understand everything that has to be anticipated and prepared for in smaller, incremental steps along the way leading up to the big day. It doesn't just magically happen all at once. Of all of the events and milestones that we experience in our lives, only one is guaranteed, and it will be the last event of your life. You already know what it is. The other major life event that runs a close parallel to funerals is weddings.

Comparing Weddings with Funerals

For people who are planning a beautiful wedding, the thought of comparing it to a funeral may not be very appealing, but consider how much they are alike. Both are rites of passage, the wedding represents the death of two single people as they move forward, into a new life as a couple.

The funeral represents the death of the physical body as the person's soul, or spirit moves forward to an afterlife of some type. If you have ever planned a wedding but not a funeral, then planning a funeral won't be so hard when you do. Weddings and funerals are so similar, that in some places, there are professional planning services that specialize in both. Both have traditionally taken place in the same church or chapel locations.

The following comparison chart shows some similarities between weddings and funerals.

Weddings:	Funerals:
Marriage license	Death certificate
Selecting a date and location	Shorter notice
Officiant	Officiant
Music/vocalist	Music/vocalist
Ceremony	Scattering/viewing
Groomsmen/bridesmaids	Pallbearers

Tuxedo/dress	Burial suit
Announcement/invitations	Obituary
Limousine	Hearse
Flowers	Flowers
Best wishes cards	Condolence cards
Theme and colors	Casket/floral color and design
Service folders/itinerary	Service folders/itinerary
Toast/honors	Eulogy
Reception	Reception
Honeymoon	Cemetery
Thank you notes	Thank you notes

The only real difference between the two is of course, the outcome and the destination. I have never heard of anyone having a sendoff shower, or rehearsal dinner for a funeral but for the most part, they are very similar.

A wedding can be simple, informal and inexpensive or be very elaborate and expensive. Many people don't seem to bat an eye when it comes to weddings and planning them. It's a joyous event that hopefully, will happen only once. Maybe money is no object. Even though funerals may be similar from a ceremonial view, the reality is most people don't see them as a joyous event.

Most people don't want to talk about them, let alone plan for one, especially for their own. Regardless, your death is certain, will happen only once, and you will definitely "use" your funeral. The same guarantee cannot be made for marriage.

Most any funeral director, estate planner or life insurance agent will have a similar conversation with you about all of the other aspects of your life that you have insured and are planning for. You insure your car and hope that you never get in a wreck or park under the wrong tree. You insure your house and hope that it never catches fire or gets broken into. The same applies with health, travel and mortgage insurance, etc. You plan and save for an array of unforeseen events and emergencies that may or may not happen, so why wouldn't you want to plan for and insure the one thing that definitely is going to happen?

At almost all of the funeral homes I have worked at, they pretty much had this same conversation with all families, both in person and in printed marketing materials. The big question after receiving the news that a loved one has died is "now what?" and this is where things get complicated and stressful for those who have not pre-planned. In many ways, each situation is different but there is one major thing that applies to everyone.

Death Certificates

After someone passes away and is released to a funeral home, the first order of business is obtaining a death certificate. These are usually issued at the county level and depending on various factors, can take anywhere from a few days to a few weeks. Most funeral homes assist with them, and some will deliver so you don't have to make another trip. If a death was from natural causes and was attended, usually at a hospital or nursing home, there is usually no need for an autopsy. The person is sent to a funeral home, where some of the necessary information is filled out.

This process should take only a few days, however, those sent to the medical examiner due to criminal or suspicious circumstances, may not be released to a funeral home for several days. Their death certificate won't be completed as quickly.

Some of the information on the death certificate is the same as a birth certificate. The persons full name, social security number, date and place of birth, their parent's full names, etc. In addition, it lists the persons last known address, spouse, usual occupation and the informant, or next of kin. A doctor or medical examiner will list the time, date, cause and manner of death. It's a good idea to have your loved ones birth certificate when you make arrangements so the information is readily available and all names are spelled correctly.

Prices vary from one place to another, so you will have to check with your county to find out. Where I live, they are $20 each right now, but as with everything else, the prices will increase over time. Some people need just one or a few, and other people need many. You will need a certified copy of the death certificate in order to collect on insurance policies, close accounts, or to claim other assets or an inheritance. A few places are easy and will accept a photo copy, but most won't. *From a business and legal standpoint, a person is not officially deceased until the death certificate is produced, and nothing will happen until such time.*

Make a list of places that will require a certified copy, this may include; Medicaid, DSHS, Veterans Administration and other government agencies, life insurance agents, investment/stock brokers, attorney's, retirement funds, and bank accounts, just to name a few. The state I live in provides one free for veterans with a red stamp on it that says "FOR VA USE ONLY." In my experience, the magic number has been five. You may need more or less but this seems to be a common amount.

Informant

The informant is the person who will be handling the decedent's affairs, at least for the purpose of obtaining the death certificates. It's usually the same person who is named as the executor or executrix, though I have seen some exceptions. This does not have to be a family member. It's usually the next of kin, but depending on the situation, could be a relative, friend or life partner, or a social worker that handles the affairs of disabled adults.

It's best to decide who this person is before the need arises. This is another source of family squabbles over who will be in charge of making arrangements and settling an estate when no plans have been made.

Other Information to Record

If you haven't already, now is the time to start writing things down and getting your thoughts organized. You can even go so far as to write your own obituary and eulogy. If you don't want to do that, then having as much information recorded as possible will help your family to do so after you pass away.

Think about the major things in your life such as family history, childhood, marriage, children, grand-children and other family tree information. Who do you want to have listed as survivors in your eulogy and obituary? How about your career, education, hobbies, organizations, military service, and all the places you've lived? In addition, record special memories, life events, milestones, accomplishments, awards, and anything else that you would like to be remembered for.

Even if you make official pre-arrangements at a funeral home and/or cemetery, you should still write down the details in the same place as your other personal information. The contract will name the major things like burial or cremation, what type of casket or urn, and whether or not it is revocable, but won't specify most of the details of your service. They may or may not already be decided at the time you pre-arrange. You will still need to decide your other preferences and wishes. As I mentioned earlier, some funeral homes will provide you with a planning guide that you can write in, or you can simply write in a notebook, or create an electronic document.

Many funeral home websites have a downloadable version that you can print out and use, even if you don't use that particular funeral home. Include the name and address of the funeral home and cemetery you plan to use in your notes, even though it will also be stated on the contract. Death causes survivors to become scatter brained and the more that is planned and recorded, the better everyone can stay on top of what needs to be handled.

Other things to write down include floral preferences, what type of flowers do you want? Do you want them in a spray on your casket lid or upright on a stand next to your casket or urn? Do you hate roses but love carnations? Who will be the pall bearers? If you're planning for cremation, you can still name honorary pall bearers. Do you desire any particular readings or scriptures that are special to you? How about having balloons, butterflies or doves released? Do you want fireworks set off? Some funeral homes and other services offer this option, but not all do so find out before finalizing any plans.

What type of music do you want played? Do you want in person singers or choir, or will it be recorded music? Is there a particular version of certain songs that you want? Make sure your survivors know who the correct artist is so they don't select a different version. Do you want a DVD made of your service to send to friends and relatives that could not attend? Do you want picture boards set up at your service? Start assembling photos and other memento's that you want included in this and let your family know where they are.

Do you want memorial donations to be sent to a particular organization or charity? Make sure you list the name and address of the recipient(s). Make a list of people to contact. The same concept applies to organizations and clubs who will need to be contacted, especially if they will be participating in your services such as military or fraternal organizations. This may sound easy with today's social media, but many older people are not online and would prefer to be contacted directly. I have spoken with several families who got in fights because someone posted a death on social media before all of the family members and close friends had been contacted.

Additional and Third Party Expenses

As you complete your arrangements at the funeral home, you will have the option to add extra funds to your contract to pay for additional items that are not directly provided by the funeral home. These other expenses include extra flowers, obituaries, death certificates, money to pay the pastor, singers and travel expenses if your casket will be shipped to another location, etc. Funeral homes cannot and do not control these other industries, therefore, cannot directly quote exact prices or guarantee anything. There are many variables to consider, and only an estimate can be made in anticipating them.

The most common amount I have seen placed into these accounts is around 10% of the total contract costs. Some places have limits, generally 15%, (having more than that may look suspicious during an audit).

10-15% may not cover everything, but again, it's better to have most, or even some of it than none of it. This extra amount will add a few dollars to the contract amount but by paying over time, it's much more affordable than having to pay all at once during an already stressful time. Nothing escapes inflation.

I have met with countless families over the years that did not anticipate, or plan for these additional expenses because their loved one had pre-planned so many years ago, and they assumed it was all taken care of. As I have mentioned several times throughout this book, it is important that you check into the affairs of anyone you will be making plans for.

Find out if they planned for any extras or just the basics, and if it will be enough when the time comes. If you decide that you have ample resources to cover your final expenses and you don't officially pre-plan at a funeral home or cemetery, make sure that you leave your survivors enough, AND immediate access to funds to cover these and other surprises that may surface as they go through this process. It doesn't do any good if nobody can get to it. Some things can be dealt with and paid for down the road, but other things must be taken care of immediately.

Obituaries

Obituaries are very expensive, especially if they contain photos. It has become popular to include two photos, one of when the decedent was young and a more recent one. Some funeral homes assist families with obituaries and some don't. It really helps if it's already done, or mostly done, when the time comes. One funeral home I worked at stopped helping people with them because it was so time consuming, and they had become a middle man to many family squabbles and miscommunications. Many families didn't have them done or have enough funds to cover them, and they were hard to collect on after the services.

A funeral home can help you submit it to the newspaper, most of which is now done electronically, but it's your responsibility to write it and have enough funds to cover it if there isn't already money allotted for it in the contract. Some families write the obituary beforehand so that people can find out where and when the service is. Others write it afterwards in cases where there is no service, or the services were private and the family did not want the details disclosed.

Other Surprises to Anticipate

During the three weeks we spent clearing out our mother's apartment, we did not once eat a home cooked meal. It wasn't possible with what we had to do, people coming and going and all of the moving, delivering and cleaning.

We spent the entire time eating out and ordering in. I did not keep track at the time, but looking back, it was probably close to $500. Plus all of the fuel costs, vehicle title transfer fee for her car, and lost wages as I left my job when she called to tell me that she only had a few months left.

Before this phone call, I just moved to another part of town to be close to the college I was scheduled to start in a few weeks. But when that call came, everything changed. I dropped everything. That was my big "now what?" moment. We were able to pay for all of these things because I was on her checking account and had immediate access. I wouldn't have been able to pay for any of it on my own.

Will your family be coming from other areas? Where will they stay and for how long? Can they afford the airfare and motel expenses? It would be wise to plan for these and other needs long beforehand. I lived away from home for 13 years and most of my return trips for funerals were paid for by my family, otherwise it just wouldn't have happened. Regardless of your circumstances and plans, I promise you there will be unexpected surprises and expenses. It's better to plan for "whatever" and "what if" than nothing at all.

Special Requests and Wishes

In addition to the standard information your survivors will need, if you have any special or unusual requests, wishes or circumstances, you will need to specify how you want them handled. If nobody knows about them then they will not get handled accordingly. Nothing will magically get done by itself. You need to take the appropriate action to ensure that all of your wishes go as planned. Have you noticed that I don't get very far into any given topic without a horror story popping up?

Horror Story

I met with a man who had five grown children. His youngest son spent most of his adult life in and out of jail because of drug problems.

The rest of the family had pretty much given up on him and moved on with their lives. This man was adamant that they were not to hold his memorial service until his son got out of jail. He wanted all five of them present and he knew that his other children would not honor his wishes.

To ensure this didn't happen, he arranged for his attorney to keep his ashes and withhold their inheritances until they were all five present. Nothing was to be removed from his home or paid out until this time. Needless to say, this caused major family problems. This was a very unusual situation and this man took the steps that would be necessary to ensure his wishes were honored.

Another Horror Story

One of my Army buddies experienced a volatile situation with his large family. His grandmother knew that there was going to be big trouble after she died. The family fights had been raging for years. She specifically stated in her will that nothing was to happen for three months after her death. After the funeral was over, nobody was allowed in her home.

She made lists of who got what, and what was to happen with every detail of her estate. She arranged for her attorney to keep her house keys and to be present when the day came for everyone to come over and clean out her house. She hoped that the ninety day waiting period would calm everyone down.

A few weeks later, he went over to mow the lawn and there was broken glass all over the back porch. He called the sheriff and her attorney. He knew right away it was someone from the family. When they went inside, only certain items were missing so he knew which cousins had done it.

They were arrested and the news travelled through the family very quickly which sparked even more fights. He told me that this was the reason he joined the Army and moved away. I never would have met him if he liked his family and wanted to stay home, so I have them to thank for our long-time friendship.

More Happy Stories

I met with a woman who wants a white carnation placed on her chest before her casket is closed. When she was six years old, her father was killed in the line of duty while chasing a murder suspect. Right before they closed his casket, she impulsively pulled a white carnation from his casket spray and placed it on his chest. She never forgot that moment, and it was very important to her that she have one too. Her family was well aware of this, but she still wrote it down with her other information.

For years, I have kept the ashes of my beloved dog Sheba. I got her when I left the Army and we were inseparable for the next nine years. When I die, I will be cremated and it's my wish that we are either buried or scattered together. Isn't it funny that someone like me has not decided yet? If we are buried, the marker will have a photo of us together on it. I have also drawn a sketch of what my marker will look like and have inscribed on it, as I do not wish to have a military marker. My family and friends have been given my instructions, otherwise, how would they know?

Share and Inform

Once you are done writing everything down and you have made all of the decisions pertaining to your final, and other arrangements, it's imperative that your survivors know where this information is. Remember the family that found their grandmothers notebook buried in a drawer a few months after she died? Some people have family meetings to make sure that everyone knows what to do. Other people simply keep this information with their other important documents and tell their family where to find it.

I can't even begin to count all of the families I worked with over the years who were unaware of their loved ones wishes, and had no knowledge of where they kept anything. This adds more stress to an already stressful situation. Make sure someone knows that you have a planning guide or notebook filled with this information. It may be beneficial to have copies made so that more than one person has access to it.

Financial Information and More Legal Problems

It's very important that you protect all of your financial and other important information. Do not include actual account numbers or pin numbers in your other notes. Make sure that whoever is in charge of your affairs has this information in a safe place. Just when you thought I was done discussing legal problems, along comes more.

In most places, having someone designated as your beneficiary or power of attorney will not automatically allow them access to your accounts. They will be able to access them later, after further authorization confirms that they are allowed to do so. In the meantime, if you want your beneficiaries, or whoever else is handling your affairs to be able to access the funds for immediate use, then you will need to specifically add them to your accounts.

Horror Story

I recently met with a very distraught woman. Her husband's sudden and unexpected death was just the beginning of her nightmare. He always handled all of their finances and both his and her money went into one account....HIS account. She was not able to access these funds and could not pay for anything. She didn't even have a basic cash flow to hold her over until the first of the month. She had to call social security to stop her checks from being automatically deposited.

The change would occur the following month but did not help her now. She also couldn't get into his smart phone because she didn't know the four digit pass code. All the vehicle titles were in his name only, so she couldn't sell one of their vehicles or get a title loan. This couple had maintained separate everything, including last names. She was also unable to log into his online shopping accounts and social media. Her life froze in an instant.

By the time she got everything settled, she was several months behind on the house payments and other bills. She had to use all of their savings and his life insurance to catch up on all of the debts and bills. There was nothing left and she had to sell the house, motor home and his truck in order to recoup the losses and have money to live on until she figured out what her next move was. If she had been on his accounts like most married people are, none of this would have happened. She would have been able to take care of everything at the time of need.

This woman found out the hard way that being married does not automatically entitle you to access anything that is in your spouse's name only. You cannot just call any bank, cell phone carrier, or other business and say "Hey, I am John Doe's wife, he died and I need to get into his accounts." It's not happening, at least not right away. Anyone can call and claim to be a spouse or child. Companies must protect their clients and themselves from fraud and legal problems.

This scenario applies to other family members as well. You must specifically add people to your accounts in order for them to have immediate access. Otherwise, they will have to go to court. Different states have different laws pertaining to these types of situations. Find out what they are and take all possible pre-cautions to avoid them.

In addition to financial information, make sure someone has access to your online pass codes to social media, shopping sites, etc. and your computer and cell phone. My mother left me all of this information, and I was able to log in and cancel everything without any of the companies even knowing that she passed away, or that it wasn't her logging in.

Keep this information with your other important documents such as titles, deeds, insurance policies, and other financial and legal documents.

In Summary

Planning for a funeral or memorial service is not much different than planning for any other major life event. The sooner you begin making plans the better off your survivors will be when the time comes. Start thinking about what kind of service you want. Write it down and be sure to keep your family informed of your plans, and other matters, so they can honor your wishes when the time comes.

It's very important that if you have any special requests or unusual circumstances, that you plan ahead as much as possible. If nobody knows about them, how can they possibly honor them?

When you go to the funeral home to make your arrangements, they will walk you through their process and explain all of the options, services and products they offer so don't feel pressured to decide everything right this minute. You may never decide on all of it, and you can always update your plans as the years go by.

There will always be surprises, and unforeseen expenses, but having the bulk of it already taken care of, will make it much easier for your survivors to fill in the gaps when the time comes. This is much better than having no plans at all.

Any funeral director can tell you that there is a world of difference between families that have pre-planned and those who have not.

CHAPTER **10**

Additional Planning and Considerations

NO MATTER HOW much pre-planning anyone does, there will be things that come up along the way that cannot get resolved until after the death. Basically anything that requires a death certificate to complete.

It can be helpful to make a list of people and places that will need to be notified. This includes doctors, dentists, the optometrist, the library, magazine and other subscriptions, all financial accounts, and social security, to name a few. One reason is that you don't want to continue receiving notices that it's time for a cleaning or card renewal.

The most important reason is that you do not want your loved ones financial and personal information floating around. It's common to continue receiving someone's mail long after they are gone. Criminals will use any information they can to gain access to accounts of any kind. Make it a point to contact everyone that was involved in the decedent's life to ensure their identity is not at risk.

Identity Theft

Death does not protect anyone from identity theft. The recently deceased are prime targets. Criminals read the obituaries looking for opportunities to find new victims. With the deceased person

114

obviously unable to notice, it may take a while for anyone to discover it. You may want to notify the three major credit bureaus of a death, even if that person did not have any credit cards or bank loans.

Someone may still try to use their name or social security number, etc. I once spoke with a detective that was involved in breaking up a huge operation of cyber-crimes including identity theft. What stood out to him were several young women in their early twenties who had names such as Ethel, Mabel, and Pearl.

These names were popular a century ago. He checked to see if they had been named after a great-grandparent or other relative, but what were the chances of not one, but several having names like these? This was just the tip of the ice berg and the small detail that got them caught.

Horror Story

One family I assisted got into a big mess over their mother's fortune, while she was still alive. Their mother had Alzheimer's disease. Two of her children noticed that money was disappearing from her accounts. Another family member, under the guise of "taking care" of her, was using her money to pay for things like a new car, breast augmentation surgery, rent, utilities and a storage shed. This person had forged dozens of documents. The other family members immediately filed a lawsuit and won.

They realized they had waited too long to take control of her financial and legal affairs, take her car away, and place her in assisted living. The documented amount stolen was close to $25k. There was more, but this was just the amount they could prove. Have I already mentioned that family is the primary source of estate fraud and theft?

The Joy of Downsizing and Reorganizing

As you go about anticipating your various needs and affairs, I strongly recommend that you take care of anything now that you can. Don't wait until you die and leave it to your family, or wait until a loved one passes and then try to deal with everything at once. A major issue that many people have to deal with is household belongings and property.

For many people, it is natural to downsize as the years go by. After many decades of maintaining a nice home and yard, it's common to move to a smaller place and then into assisted living or a nursing home. But for some, they wish to remain in their homes until the very end. This is great for some people but can also be a nightmare for others, especially if you are dealing with an elderly parent who refuses to throw anything away or allow anyone else to. When they pass away, you will have the added burden of cleaning out their home. This can mean more time away from work and other obligations, and additional expenses of hauling, moving and storing. It's even more difficult when you don't live in the same town and either have to travel, or pay someone to do it.

By doing this beforehand, even partially, it will take a huge burden off when the time comes. It's often easier to deal with things in more manageable increments than to get overwhelmed all at once.

Happy Story

After placing our great-grandmother in a nursing home, my uncle arranged for everyone to come over and start going through her things. Fortunately, there was no arguing or disputes. We each got what we wanted and the rest was donated to a thrift store. When I removed my dad's high school portrait from the wall, I thought it felt kind of heavy. I removed the backing and realized that she had hidden other pictures behind it. This prompted us to look behind the others, and sure enough, many of them had other pictures behind them.

While vacuuming, my uncle noticed that the carpet in her closet had been pulled out from under the baseboard. She had valuable documents, old money and coins laid flat under it. Great hiding spot, good thing he found it.

Even though this move was well organized and everyone cooperated, it was still very exhausting, time consuming and labor intensive. She died a few months later, and we were able to celebrate her life without worrying about having a lot of additional things to do. It was already done.

Afterwards, my grandmother decided she was going to start cleaning out her own home so we didn't have to deal with it later. She gave each grandchild certain things that were special to each one of us. She was done sewing and gardening, and had somehow accumulated several dozen coffee mugs over the years.

Less than a year later, one of her legs needed to be amputated so she was glad she did this. When she died a few years later, it didn't take long to clear out her home. Both she and my great grandmother had a lot of pictures, many I had never seen before.

A few of my cousins and I had a "picture party." We went through them and made piles of the ones we wanted. We had copies made which not only allowed us to each have a set, but also serves as backup if any of us ever lose them.

Horror Story

Years ago, one of my friends called me in hysterics. Her mom stored several plastic bins containing hundreds of family pictures, under her bed. One day they pulled them out and were horrified to discover that every one of them was torn to shreds. They knew exactly who did it, and were angry because it had been over a year and they just now discovered it.

Her sister, who had always been the family troublemaker, and estranged for most of their adult lives, got in a fight with their mom during one of her many blow ups. They had not seen or heard from her since and apparently, this was her way of getting even before she left. I stopped by later that day and after she calmed down, I nicely pointed out that even though they were ripped, at least they were technically still there.

Her sister could have thrown them away or set them on fire. I helped her clear off the big dining room table, and set up for a huge repair project. She and her mom spent the next week painstakingly piecing them all back together like a puzzle, and carefully taping them on the back.

It cost over $400 to have them professionally touched up and re-printed. It wasn't the same as having the originals but was better than nothing. After this incident, her mom realized it was time to make some changes in her will and other legal matters.

Happy Story

One of my neighbors decided to deal with his mother's much needed downsizing situation in a way that was beneficial for the whole family. Their mother was becoming increasingly feeble since their father passed away a year earlier. They were worried about her going up and down the stairs. The laundry room was in the basement, which was completely full of stuff that had accumulated over the past six decades.

Their mother was adamant about staying there. They didn't want to have to force her to leave either, but the house was full of safety hazards that could not be ignored. They decided to remodel and "mama-proof" the house instead of putting her in assisted living. The first thing they did was sell her car and golf cart. They used those funds to pre-pay for her funeral, and I made sure they chose the irrevocable option just in case she did have to go into a home.

While they were cleaning out the basement, they decided it would be a good time to divide up their father's guns, tools, hunting and fishing gear. All three sons got what they wanted without conflict, and now they would not have to worry about any of it getting stolen, or injuring their mother.

They remodeled one of the upstairs bedrooms into a new bathroom and laundry room. They had the house re-wired to move the fuse box upstairs. They built a new, shorter kitchen with all new appliances featuring the latest and greatest safety features, and then locked the basement door, as there was no need for her to ever go down there again.

This project allowed her to stay there, until she died three years later. The cost was pennies compared to what it would have been for assisted living. When they sold her house, they got quite a bit more than they would have without the upgrades. They were able to receive an inheritance from her estate, and didn't have the extra burden of having to clean out and haul everything away afterwards.

If they hadn't done this, they would have had to sell the house and everything in it to pay for her long term care, and there would have been nothing left when she passed. They also would have had to pay for her funeral expenses.

Happy Story

Another man I worked with not only made his funeral arrangements, but settled most of his own estate while he was still alive. He lived an amazing life and built quite an empire, but now at eighty-three, the cancer was back for the third time and he realized it was time to start winding down. He was taught from an early age, the concept of not putting all your eggs in one basket.

He had dozens of accounts, investments, businesses and properties in several states. He arranged his will so that each of his three children would receive equal shares of everything. Problem was, with all of his holdings, there were some legal issues that his kids would have to deal with after he was gone. There was a boundary dispute with one of his larger properties, and none of his kids or other relatives were interested in any of the businesses he owned.

He spent the next year selling, closing and consolidating his assets and holdings. He forfeited the disputed land and sold it all to the neighbor. It was worth far more than expected so that was a blessing in disguise. He moved everything into fewer, more manageable accounts. He was relieved to know that his kids would not have to deal with any of it after he was gone.

Another Happy Story

One woman I know was in a similar situation. She has always been the family historian and has a large collection of heirloom items that she had received after the deaths of several relatives.

She also received several inheritances. As is so common with many families, she has two relatives who were always a thorn in her side. They had been squabbling for years over several items they felt they should have received, and the money....always the money.

She also has two adult children, both with functional limitations who aren't able to make any legal decisions, or defend themselves against the other family members. This woman made the choice to give several items and some money to these two people. They accepted. She basically paid them to go away. If they were nicer, it would have been a lot more. She then updated her will and other legal matters to protect her children so that after she passes away, nobody else has any grounds to dispute her wishes.

Horror Story

Another family I worked with had to deal with a terrible situation that never should have happened. Two adult siblings inherited some acreage from their mother. It was prime and valuable riverfront property. They planned to eventually build on it, but for now, put in a single wide trailer that would hold them over until they could finalize their plans. Life happened and they ended up placing their former step-father in it, for what they thought would just be a year or less.

They didn't realize at first that he had such advanced dementia, and became extremely difficult to deal with. He never cleaned or threw anything away, and began accumulating animals. He was unable to care for, or contain them and they wandered onto other people's property, destroying their gardens and landscaping, and attacking their pets.

Because of his age, they were unable to simply evict him and he refused to budge. They spent the next four years going to court, and fighting with several agencies that deal with elder care, trying to get him placed in assisted living. He would not allow them to clean or remove anything.

It consumed their entire lives and finances. Eventually, it got so bad the trailer was condemned and the man was forcibly removed from it after it caught fire twice. Almost all of the animals had to be euthanized because of skin diseases and behavioral safety risks. They were also sued by several neighbors.

When it was all over, these two siblings lost everything and ended up selling the property just to break even from the legal proceedings. The trailer was a complete loss and their plans to build a nice family, summer cabin were gone. If they had been honest with themselves about their step-fathers mental state, the end result would have been much different.

Non-Monetary Estates

You may feel that these types of situations don't apply to you because you don't have an estate, per se, or any family to speak of. As I have mentioned before, you don't have to be rich in order to have a problem. Everyone has an estate, even if it's just literally the clothes on your back, and the plastic watch you bought at a thrift store that doesn't work anymore. If you died tomorrow, what will your roommate or landlord do with all of your things? What about pictures, documents and sentimental items that cannot be replaced?

In many places, it's illegal to just throw out someone's belongings because they died and roommates and landlords don't know how to contact their family. Landlords can get into all kinds of legal and financial messes after the death of a tenant. Laws differ from place to place. Most rental documents require an emergency contact. Make sure your landlord and roommates know who to call if something happens to you.

Horror Story

One landlord I spoke with had to leave one of his properties untouched for almost two years. The tenant was found dead under suspicious circumstances in another location. He was not allowed to touch or move anything during the investigation. He didn't receive the rent for those months. He was sucked into a tornado of grief with the insurance company, the tenant's family and the police. Before it was over, he had to sell one of his other properties to recoup the loss from this one. He eventually received a settlement to cover the lost rent, but it did not cover the other expenses and problems it created.

Other Things to Consider

If you're geographically isolated and/or emotionally estranged from your relatives, there are still steps you can take to protect your roommates and landlord, and to ensure that your belongings get to the right person. Leave written instructions describing what you want them to do with your stuff. It's easy if it's just clothes and they can throw them out. But it must be made known if you have any important items that need to be returned to your uncle that you have not seen in ten years.

You may have relatives that you don't like, or haven't been in contact with for a long time, but you still want to ensure that certain items are given to them after you die. Consider photographing items and leaving a detailed explanation of what is to be done with them.

Write down the contact info of relatives and other people that would need to know about your passing. Remember my friend that had to legally disown his brother because he wasn't able to make sound decisions? That's not all he did. He also realized that most of his social contacts are unaware of each other. A lot of people know him but don't know each other.

He typed up an explanation of what needed to happen if he died or became incapacitated. He added a list of contact information and gave a copy to his landlord, a neighbor, his boss, pastor, several friends, cousins, and veteran groups that he belonged to.

Horror Story

I recently spoke with a young man who had just been placed into an apartment by a veteran organization, after being homeless for six months. He had lived with a roommate for several years that paid for half of everything. One day, his roommate went out for a bike ride and was killed in an accident. Within a few weeks, he could no longer pay the rent or utilities. As if the loss of his friend wasn't bad enough, he had to give away his cats and abandon most of his belongings because he had no place to put them. It happened that fast.

Four Legged Survivors

Speaking of cats, if something happened to you tonight, who would know where your pets are? Who would take them? If you live alone or don't have any family nearby, it's important to plan for your pets in addition to all of the other necessary arrangements.

Just as you would find a pet sitter while on vacation, you need to make plans for someone to come and get them, especially if they are locked inside your residence. I recently saw a wallet sized card at a pet store that was similar to a medical notification card. It had a bright red border with the title "I HAVE PETS AT HOME ALONE," then had the address and contact info down below.

This is a wonderful idea and may make a difference in whether or not your pets get rescued or adopted in the event of your passing, or serious disability. What if it takes several days for someone to get to them? If you don't have family, find a trusted friend or neighbor that can help.

Lost or Damaged Documents

This is a problem that can usually be solved pretty easily. Again, don't wait until after a death, or other crisis has occurred before you realize that your mom has lost the title to the motor home, or your dad spilled coffee on his insurance papers, and did not clean it up in time to save them.

With today's technology, it is much faster and easier to keep multiple copies of documents in an electronic format. But sometimes, a hard copy is needed. In addition, many hard copy documents that were produced many decades ago may never have been scanned or copied into an electronic format. Another reason it is so important to stay on top of everything and update as needed.

It can take time and cost money to replace and/or transfer documents. Property deeds, vehicle titles, insurance policies, tax and other legal documents, and military documents, just to name a few. As the years go by, we all get busy with life and things get lost. Items and documents get shoved into boxes and drawers, especially during moves. We promise ourselves that we will get to it later when we have time. If it has been "awhile" since you saw important documents or items, it's time to find or replace them.

I recently met with an elderly veteran who is a widower. He assured me that all of his affairs were in order, but I didn't believe it based on the condition of his home. He was a stage five hoarder. While we were cleaning his house, I found his will and advanced directives crumpled up in the back of the spice cabinet, covered with BBQ rub.

He was right. His legal matters were not only current and valid but smelled wonderful too! We found other important documents scattered throughout the house, and convinced him to let us put them all together in one of his six briefcases. When we went back a week later, the briefcase was in the back room closet, under a box full of old, smelly fishing tackle.

In Summary

Someone I was discussing this chapter with thought I should leave it out because identity theft, parents with dementia, and cleaning out houses has nothing to do with dying. I beg to differ, yes it does. Please don't think that your death, the events leading up to it, and the ensuing aftermath won't affect anyone because it will.

Sometimes one small detail can cause an avalanche of events and issues that are hard to see at first. Somebody has to deal with it regardless of your circumstances or financial status. Do what you can to minimize this burden on whoever will be handling your affairs, or be affected by your death in any way.

Be honest with yourself about your family situation. Don't deny that your parents are becoming feeble or memory impaired, a sibling is a criminal, or a cousin plans to sue your children the minute your gone. Family, legal and financial situations all intertwine at some point, anticipate as much as you can and then take the appropriate action to avoid or solve it.

I already mentioned this in the introduction and will say it again because it is so true and so important.......

In most circumstances, it's not what you do or don't HAVE, but WHO is handling it, and HOW it's handled, that determines the outcome of any given situation.

Afterword

THE DAY I started writing this book, I taped a piece of notebook paper to the end of my desk and dated it. Over the next several months that I spent writing and editing this book, I kept a list of everyone I knew that experienced a death in their family. This list did not include people that I just heard about, or had no other connection to. These were people that I know personally.

Eleven friends, co-workers, relatives, and myself all experienced a loss. Most were expected, but a few were not. As I was finishing the last chapter, I took a break and went to an outdoor sportsman's event. I ran into one of my backpacking friends. We chatted for a while, and I told him about this book and the seminars I have been conducting.

The last thing he said to me was "we need to catch up soon." I promised to personally deliver a signed copy. Three weeks later, he almost made it to the top of a mountain when he collapsed and died, right there on the trail.

Death has long been referred to as "the great equalizer" and it's the truth. It doesn't matter who you are, how you live, your political or religious beliefs, your socio-economic status, race, nationality, health etc. etc. Every single one of us is going to die, we always have and we always will. There is no way out of it. The worst thing anyone can do is live in denial, and not plan for it.

It was difficult to keep this book as short as it is. I could easily go back and add in dozens of horror stories. As I wrote each one, several more came to mind. You get the point with the ones I included.

Please do not create, or star in one of my horror stories.

CPSIA information can be obtained
at www.ICGtesting.com
Printed in the USA
BVHW030717111022
649115BV00007B/113